NORTH EASTERN RAILWAY

– HISTORICAL MAPS –

R.A. COOK and K. HOOLE

RAILWAY AND CANAL HISTORICAL SOCIETY

First published in 1975

This Revised second edition published in 1991
by the
Railway and Canal Historical Society
Registered Office: Fron Fawnog, Hafod Road, Gwernymynydd, Mold, Clwyd CH7 5JS

© 1991 Railway and Canal Historical Society

ISBN 0 901461 13 X

Design Malcolm Preskett
Printed in England by
Hobbs the Printers of Southampton

RAILWAY & CANAL HISTORICAL SOCIETY

FOUNDED 1954   INCORPORATED 1967

The Railway & Canal Historical Society was founded in 1954. Its objects are to bring together all those seriously interested in the history of transport, with particular reference to railways, waterways, and all matters associated with them: to encourage historical research; and to promote a high standard of publication – in the Society's Journal or elsewhere. While railways and canals form the basis of the Society, it recognizes that a serious study of their history is often inseparable from a study of associated modes of transport, such as river navigations, roads, docks, coastal shipping, and ferries.

For many, the biggest benefit which membership brings is the contact with others having similar interests. In addition to local Groups, for members living in particular areas,

a recent extension has been the formation of groups catering for particular interests – road history, docks and coastal shipping, and tramroads. Members also have the advantage of regular issues of the Society's Journal and Bulletin as well as access to the extensive Research Index and to the Research Fund.

Full details of membership will gladly be sent on application to the Membership Secretary: R J Taylor, 16 Priory Court, Berkhamsted, Herts HP4 2DP.

A full list of the Society's publications is available on application to the RHCS Sales Officer, 23 Beanfield Avenue, Coventry CV3 6NZ, from whom the publications themselves can also be obtained.

Contents

Preface

THE PURPOSE of this series of maps is to show the building up of the North Eastern Railway system until its identity was lost in the 1923 grouping. The key map at the beginning of the series shows the areas covered by each of the main maps, which are numbered from north to south, and from west to east. More complex districts are the subject of detailed maps, which are indicated on the key map, and cross-referenced on the main area maps; conversely, the detail maps are referred back to the main area maps.

As far as is known, in an area of such complexity, the maps show every section of line owned, or worked, by the company for regular public traffic, although short NER-owned spurs, or sidings, connecting with private company's lines and works have been omitted for clarity, even though these existed in large numbers. Notwithstanding this, it is freely admitted that there may be omissions or positional errors. An 'out-of-scale' approach has been adopted in an attempt to avoid confusion where actual sites or routes lie close together. It is for this reason also that no attempt has been made to show intermediate stations etc.

The earliest dates shown are those on which each section of line carried public traffic. However, with many of the early companies, whose main concern was to transport minerals, it is impossible to differentiate between formal and public openings. In these instances the generally accepted dates have been used, it being by no means certain that public traffic was not carried following – or even attached to – the formal opening train.

Where known, the type of traffic carried is indicated by a prefix before the date. A second, or third, prefix indicates the opening to the public for other types of traffic. Due to limitations of space, only the last two digits of the year are shown. The maps, however, are limited in period to 1825–1920, so that no confusion can arise; e,g, 3-3-47 is 3 March 1847, and 1-6-05 is 1 June 1905. During the last twenty years of the company's separate existence it was customary for the term 'freight' to replace the more generally used 'goods', but in an attempt to avoid additional confusion the more usual term has been adopted for the prefix notation, *viz*:

m – coals or minerals   g – goods
p – passengers

In many instances the length of line opened for other traffic does not coincide with the previously opened stretch; in those cases, to avoid the complications attendant on a multiplicity of dates, no additional dates are shown.

A list of lines which have, to date, no authenticated opening dates is appended, together with whatever information is available at the time of writing. Any data which would reduce the length of the list would be appreciated by the author. Where only an approximate period for the opening of the line is known, this is indicated in the tabulation, and is shown on the maps as: e.g. c1850.

Junction names have been extracted from later official company records including the NER *Working Timetables and Appendices* for 1898 and 1918, and the LNER *Working Timetable* for 1924. Although space precludes the showing of all named junctions, care has been taken to avoid the use of unofficial names. The details of Acts have been taken from the *Index to Local and Personal Acts 1801–1947*, and the Royal Assent dates from the most authoritative sources available.

First edition   R. A. Cook 1975
(amended 1990)

Acknowledgements

IN ANY work concerning this company, initial acknowledgement must be made to the official history of the company by W. W. Tomlinson, whose work gives the broadest possible base for any work concerning the North Eastern Rly; this despite the historical content being somewhat sparse after 1880.

I am deeply indebted to my co-author, and fellow member, Ken Hoole, for his excellent and detailed historical introduction to the company. His intimate knowledge has been invaluable in the compilation of the maps, whilst his ready response to queries on dates and sites in the more complicated areas, and his valued comments and painstaking checking of the maps during the months it has taken to put this work together, have been greatly appreciated.

I am also indebted to Mr C. R. Clinker for access to, and information from, his authoritative work *Clinker's Register of Closed Passenger Stations and Goods Depots in England, Scotland and Wales*; for much additional information used in the compilation of the Act section, and for the loan of Working Timetables and Appendices from his collection.

Grateful acknowledgement is also due to Mr D. Garnett, who had made a tremendous contribution by supplying a considerable amount of detailed information and diagrams from his collection of Airey's and Railway Clearing House maps and junction diagrams, and from other maps in his collection.

Acknowledgement is also due to Dr A. L. Barnett for his checking of the Act section, and the maps in the south Yorkshire area; to Mr J. C. Dean, for checking, comments, and information in the Newcastle and Tynemouth areas; to David Joy, who has kindly checked the Leeds and Methley area maps, and has supplied many previously unknown dates; and to Mr T. E. Rounthwaite, whose knowledge and help in the Cleveland area and around Shildon has been greatly appreciated.

Of the many books, periodicals and journals consulted, especial mention must be made of the North Eastern Railway Association *Express*; notably for articles by Messrs Dean and Rounthwaite, which have given detailed information in some complicated areas.

Thanks are also due to Mr D. Barlow, Archivist of the British Transport Historical Records in London, for photo-copies of documents from the Tomlinson Collection; to Dr M. J. T. Lewis, who has taken much of the finalised typing load off my shoulders; and lastly, but by no means least, to my wife Enid, who has not only put up with me over the last few months, but has assisted in the preparation of this booklet by checking my initial drafts, and by drawing the complicated crest of the company which appears on the cover.

March 1975   R. A. Cook

Preface to Revised Edition

IN ALL historical works, whatever one's chosen subject, it is ever true that yesterday's facts are today's — and indeed tomorrow's — fallacies. This work was no exception.

In compiling this revised edition, I am grateful to have had the co-operation over the intervening years of almost all those mentioned in the original work. However, it is with great personal sadness that one has to record the passing of my co-author, Ken Hoole, perhaps the most knowledgeable of North Eastern Railway historians; Charles Clinker, one of only a small number who promoted a more academic approach to serious railway historical research; and of David Garnett, best known for his studious work in connection with railway maps in general, and RCH and Airey's maps in particular.

Of those whose work over the past several years has been invaluable, especial mention must be made of fellow members Stephen Bragg, for his valued comments and his kindness in making available the results of his research work on the Ordnance Survey large-scale maps throughout the north east. To this must be added his detailed study of the railway history of the two Hartlepools, which has enhanced our knowledge of the tangled network of lines in that area, and also that of Hull. Thanks are also extended to David Joy, for his research into the mysteries of Carlisle, and also for his work on South and West Yorkshire. I am also grateful to David Tee for additional information on Carlisle, and to R. Bealby and A. E. Bennett for early corrections of the first edition.

Finally to another fellow member, Michael Cobb, whose painstaking work on both the Ordnance Survey, and many older, maps has rectified many other errors in the first edition. With any map, it is ever a fact that there is little of consequence that one can leave out, or ignore, and with his assistance over several years, combined latterly with that of Stephen Bragg, has made this edition, hopefully, far more complete and accurate than hitherto.

Of written works, due acknowledgement must be made to a handbook published by the Industrial Railway Society, *Industrial Locomotives of Durham*, one of an expanding series of extremely detailed and exhaustive works by that Society. Although primarily devoted to industrial locomotives, it has proved invaluable, and a mine of information, not only in terms of the siting of private industrial workings, but also for the many other historical details of the companies themselves, and of their railway connections.

As with the earlier work, I have, once more, to thank my wife, Enid, who has again had to tolerate an untidy accumulation of books, papers and maps strewn around the house, particularly the living room.

In the hope of making the maps more easily related to one another, the opportunity has been taken to add the continuations at the termination points of every line on each map. In redrafting the key map, the boundaries of the smaller area maps have been included, rather than present them in list form. With these smaller areas, for example, NE18a/NE18b refer to the upper and lower portions respectively of map NE18. The opportunity has also been taken to identify more of the better known rope-worked inclines, of all types, which abounded on the NER — notably on the Stanhope & Tyne. In order to make this addition more informative, the direction of the arrow alongside an incline indicates a rising gradient.

Finally, in the unfortunate absence of my co-author, his excellent précis introduction to the earlier work will remain verbatim, other than for updating, not only in the hope that he would have approved of the new work, but that it may, in part, remain a fitting memorial to him, and to his work on the area he served so well over a period of many years.

During my years as a tool designer, one was always conscious of the role played by the checkers — the long-stop in cricketing parlance. A work of this nature is, if anything, even more complicated. Despite care in the drafting, there is ever a case of familiarity breeding contempt, and it is at this stage that checking becomes a vital necessity. In this respect I am extremely grateful to both Stephen Bragg and Michael Cobb for their diligence in checking both the siting and the content of the maps, together with their helpful suggestions.

R. A. Cook.

Historical Introduction to the North Eastern Railway

THE NORTH Eastern Railway was fourth in size of the British railway companies, serving an area of north eastern England bounded by the coastline in the east, the River Humber in the south, and the Tweed in the north. Except for a trio of lines penetrating as far west as Tebay, Penrith and Carlisle, the North Eastern was contained east of the Pennines, making it a compact company serving mainly the counties of Yorkshire, Durham and Northumberland.

The North Eastern was formed in 1854 by the amalgamation of three companies – the York & North Midland, the York, Newcastle & Berwick, and the Leeds Northern: these three had in turn absorbed, or had developed from, companies dating back to the 1830s and 1840s. The York & North Midland was the line ruled over by George Hudson, promoted to provide a route from York to London (Euston Square) by joining the North Midland Railway at Altofts Junction, north of Normanton. By extensions, leases, and amalgamations it obtained access to the coast at Bridlington, Scarborough, and Whitby, and to the developing port of Hull on the north bank of the Humber. The oldest constituent was the Leeds & Selby, opened in 1834, but the Y&NM also included the Whitby & Pickering of 1835/6, originally a horse-worked line, but converted to locomotive operation after the opening of a branch from Rillington to Pickering in 1845.

The York, Newcastle & Berwick was also an amalgamation of lines to form a through route from York to Berwick, with numerous branches east and west of the main line: many of these, too, dated from the 1830s and 1840s. The Leeds Northern started life as the Leeds & Thirsk Railway, opened throughout in 1849 and renamed in the same year, when it envisaged extending north-eastwards to Northallerton and Stockton, reached in 1852.

The amalgamation of 1854 still left a number of companies outside the NER net, but these were taken over as the company continued to grow. However, not all these companies owned locomotives and/or rolling stock, as they had been worked by the NER from the outset. The final amalgamation between the NER and the Hull & Barnsley Railway was a prelude to the 1923 grouping.

Most of the lines covered by the maps were authorised by an Act of Parliament, although some connecting curves and minor lines were built under General Powers and cannot therefore be found and identified in any Act. A few other lines, notably the Stanhope & Tyne, were built using wayleaves to compensate the landowners for passing over their land, and thus again there is no authorising Act.

In 1863 the North Eastern took over the Stockton & Darlington Railway, by that time stretching across North Yorkshire and County Durham, from Saltburn on the coast to Consett in the hills of north west Durham. This had developed from the world's first steam worked public railway, opened formally from Witton Park to Stockton on 27 September 1825. When it was opened, the Stockton & Darlington had only one locomotive, and this worked the inaugural train from Shildon: north west of Shildon the line was carried over two ridges of high land on rope-worked inclines, with a horse-worked level stretch between them.

Many of the earthworks of the original line still exist, together with some bridges: the most notable bridge, that over the River Skerne at Darlington, is still in use for rail traffic, and it is possible to travel over parts of the 1825 line by using the Darlington – Bishop Auckland and Darlington – Saltburn diesel railcar services.

Although the North Eastern had a virtual monopoly between the Humber and the Tweed, there were a few small lines which remained independent, namely the Alne & Easingwold, the North Sunderland, the Derwent Valley Light, and the Nidd Valley Light.

These all carried passengers at one time. A number of colliery companies in County Durham and Northumberland also operated passenger services, and although the trains were primarily for miners travelling to and from their work, they were also available to the public. The service at Ashington Colliery in Northumberland continued until the 1960s, operated latterly by the National Coal Board. The coaches used on this service were largely North Eastern vehicles, some of which have been retained for preservation at Beamish Open Air Museum in County Durham.

Another unusual feature of operation in the north east was the use of the main line company's tracks by mineral trains operated by colliery engines, wagons and crews. These services were long established and were originally provided to avoid duplication of trucks between colliery and shipping point. Notable examples were those between Penshaw North and Sunderland operated by the Lambton, Hetton & Joicey group of collieries, and between Boldon Colliery and Tyne Dock operated by the Harton Coal Company. Some of these services continued well into BR days, operated by the National Coal Board.

At the time the North Eastern was formed in 1854, a new route from York to the south was just being established. Instead of travelling via the main line of the York & North Midland to Altofts Junction, and then forward from Normanton via the North Midland, a connection was opened between the Y&NM at Burton Salmon and the Lancashire & Yorkshire at Knottingley. Near Arksey, north of Doncaster, the L&Y made an end-on junction with the Great Northern, and thus it was possible for trains from Doncaster and the south to reach York. This route continued in use as the main line until 1871 when, with the opening of links between the Great Northern at Shaftholme Junction and Selby, and between Barlby (north of Selby) and York, the present main line came into being.

Further north the original main line ran via Ferryhill, Leamside, Penshaw, Washington and Pelaw, to Gateshead, over a route built up by the Newcastle & Darlington Junction, Durham Junction, Stanhope & Tyne, and Brandling Junction companies. At first the route between Washington and Pelaw was via Brockley Whins, but a direct line between these two points was opened in 1849. Between 1868 and 1872 connecting links were put in between Gateshead and Newton Hall (north of Durham), and between Relly Mill (south of Durham) and Ferryhill, completing the main line as we know it today. Both the old main line routes described still exist but are little used, although they do provide an alternative in the event of the main line being blocked.

Many of the colliery and county branches have had their track removed, and in some places they have been converted into country walks and bridlepaths, whilst similar alterations are in hand at other locations. For the Stockton & Darlington 150th anniversary celebrations in 1975, clearance work was carried out on some of the badly overgrown portions of the original route of 1825, from which trains were withdrawn over 130 years before!

Under an agreement of 1862, the North Eastern worked East Coast expresses over the North British line from Berwick to Edinburgh, and thus the haulage between London and Edinburgh was shared between the Great Northern and the North Eastern. The change of engines took place at York, although North Eastern engines were also changed at Newcastle where, until 1906 and the opening of the King Edward Bridge, all trains had to reverse.

The main flow of mineral and goods traffic was to the East Coast for shipment, and the North Eastern was well provided with branches running east to west, serving the various ports. Some of these lines had been built with rope-worked inclines, but with the introduction of more powerful engines it was possible to convert them to locomotive operation. However, some inclines remained in operation until fairly recently, particularly on the Tanfield branch, and part of the Stanhope & Tyne route. Most of the Stanhope & Tyne inclines were abandoned in the 1940s and 1950s, but Waldridge incline, near Chester-le-Street, continued in operation to bring down coal, whilst at the south west end of the line trains continued to run over the wild moorland line to Weatherhill, past the decaying railway village of Waskerley. Another remote line, also traversing wild moorland country, was that to the ironstone mines at Rosedale. This involved wagons being hauled up the long Ingleby incline, which was as steep as 1 in 5 at the top, with locomotive haulage from the summit to Rosedale, where there was a small locomotive shed.

Appointed Locomotive Superintendent on the formation of the NER in 1854 was Edward Fletcher, who had been brought up with locomotives. He was born in 1807 and as a youth he was apprenticed to George Stephenson: he was on the footplate of the *Invicta* when it opened the Canterbury & Whitstable Railway in 1830, and he was involved in the trials of the *Rocket* before it was sent to the Rainhill Trials. In 1845 he was appointed Locomotive Superintendent of the Newcastle & Darlington Junction Railway (later to become the York & Newcastle, and eventually the York, Newcastle & Berwick) and thus was in direct line for the post with the enlarged company at the amalgamation.

His designs were sturdy and reliable, and under his charge the North Eastern became notable for its many varieties of locomotives. Repairs and rebuilding were carried out at the various works at Gateshead, Tyne Dock, Leeds, Hartlepool, etc, and each works was allowed a large amount of latitude, so that an engine dealt with at one works bore little resemblance to one of the same class dealt with at another works. Contractors supplying new engines were also allowed to use their own ideas to develop the main dimensions laid down by Fletcher, so that it was extremely obvious which engines came from which contractors.

Fletcher is best remembered for his Class 901 2-4-0s and his Class 398 0-6-0s, but there were other classes built in quantity. Many of these, built in the 1870s, worked long enough to become LNER property in 1923, and some of the 0-4-4 tank engines rebuilt as 0-6-0Ts between 1900 and 1921 lasted well into BR days.

Fortunately 910, of Class 901, the largest of

the 2-4-0s, was preserved after it had been withdrawn in 1925 and, after taking part in the 1925 Centenary Procession, it was placed in York Museum: it will be on display in the National Railway Museum.

Fletcher retired in 1882 at the age of 75, with a pension of £1,200 a year, and he was succeeded by Alexander McDonnell from the Great Southern & Western Railway of Ireland. Unfortunately the North Eastern footplate men took a dislike to his engines, and his position became so untenable that he resigned in 1884. During his period in office he designed two classes of engine – a 4-4-0 (Class 38) with a strong likeness to his 4-4-0s in Ireland, and an 0-6-0 (Class 59). The last 4-4-0 was withdrawn early in 1923, but all the 0-6-0s became LNER property and the last was not withdrawn for scrapping until December 1930.

Until a new Locomotive Superintendent could be appointed the department was in charge of a Committee, with the General Manager, Henry Tennant, as Chairman. As new express passenger engines were required, a design was produced for a class of 2-4-0 of which ten were built at Gateshead and ten at Darlington. These became known as the Tennant Class, but the General Manager was not a technical man and it seems very probable that the design was prepared by Wilson Worsdell, who later became Chief Mechanical Engineer of the company, although Tennant received £500 for his work!

To fill the gap left by McDonnell's departure the NER Directors appointed Thomas William Worsdell from the Great Eastern Railway, brother of the Worsdell mentioned above.

T. W. Worsdell took office on 1 September 1885 at a salary of £3,000 a year, and he immediately started a standardisation programme. His influence can be traced in all subsequent NER engines, including those which lasted on BR until 1967. His engines were notable for their clean lines, with double side windows to the cabs on the tender engines. His alphabetical system of locomotive classification was used exclusively until 1923, and side-by-side with the LNER classification until 1932. From 1904 the class was displayed on the front buffer-beam and thus became familiar to anyone at all interested in locomotives, so much so that almost anyone would instantly recognise the significance of, for instance, Class R or Class Z.

T. W. Worsdell had one particular hobby-horse — two cylinder compounds — and he used this system on most of his locomotives, although in some cases he would build compound and simple engines simultaneously for purposes of comparison. Eventually 269 compound engines were built, but they were all rebuilt with two high-pressure cylinders by Wilson Worsdell after his brother had retired.

Wilson Worsdell succeeded his brother in 1890 and followed the general outline of the designs introduced by Thomas William, gradually increasing the size of his 4-4-0s, and introducing 4-6-0s and 4-4-2s for East Coast passenger work. In fact, the 4-6-0s were the first passenger engines of that type in the country. For freight and mineral traffic he built a large fleet of 0-6-0s, introducing in 1904 the P2 class with a 5ft 6in diameter boiler — 1ft 3in larger than on previous 0-6-0s. There was also the successful 0-8-0 class, some of which had piston valves (Class T) and some slide valves (Class T1), built between 1901 and 1911, and withdrawn between 1946 and 1951.

The P3 0-6-0 class, introduced in 1906, was similar to the earlier P2 design and these were built over a period of 17 years. They were actually the last standard gauge pre-grouping design of 0-6-0 to run on BR and the final five, four built by the NER and one by the LNER, were withdrawn in September 1967 when steam traction ceased on the main lines in north eastern England. One of the class has been preserved on the North Yorkshire Moors Railway under the auspices of the North Eastern Locomotive Preservation Group.

Wilson Worsdell was not a lover of his brother's compound engines, and after putting in hand a series of comparative tests he decided that they should be rebuilt as simple engines, a task not completed until 1913. During his period in office the locomotive build-ing and repair work was concentrated at Gateshead and Darlington, but even Gateshead was restricted to repairs after the completion of extensions to the works at Darlington around the time of Worsdell's retirement. Wilson Worsdell inaugurated electric traction on the NER, with the electrification in 1904 of the suburban lines in the Newcastle area, with multiple unit trains running on the third rail system, although the two electric locomotives built for working the Quayside branch were also fitted for overhead collection.

Vincent Raven succeeded Worsdell in 1910: he had been Worsdell's right-hand man for many years and he was a North Eastern man through and through. He, too, perpetuated the Worsdell outline of North Eastern engines, but he built larger engines, many with three cylinders, such as the magnificent Z (saturated) and Z1 (superheated) Atlantics, of which the first twenty were built by the North British Locomotive Co. of Glasgow in 1911. A further thirty were built at Darlington between 1914 and 1918. His largest passenger engines were the two Pacifics, completed in the final days of the NER, and a further three were built by the LNER in 1924. Unfortunately these five engines were overshadowed by the Gresley engines with the same wheel arrangement, and it was the latter class which was perpetuated by the LNER. Consequently no more North Eastern Pacifics were built, and 2400–2404 passed to the scrapheap in 1936/7. Thus the three engines built in 1924 had a life of only 12 or 13 years and they were, in fact, the first LNER built engines to be withdrawn and scrapped.

For goods traffic, Raven developed the two-cylinder T2 0-8-0, of which 120 were built, and the three-cylinder T3 0-8-0, of which only 15 were built between 1919 and 1924. The two-cylinder locomotives were particularly good engines and had the distinction of being the last 0-8-0s to run on BR. One of the T2 engines is preserved on the North Yorkshire Moors Railway, and may be joined eventually by the BR preserved T3 engine.

During World War I, Raven was released by the NER for duties at Woolwich Arsenal (for which he received a Knighthood) and in his absence his assistant, A. C. Stamer, took charge of the Locomotive Department. In this period the design was prepared for the S3 mixed-traffic 4-6-0 engines, another NER design which became well known, because the work it could perform took it to many locations outside the north east.

Raven was alive to traction developments and, in 1914, he electrified the former Stockton & Darlington, Clarence, and North Eastern lines which conveniently formed a through route from Shildon to Middlesbrough without conflicting with north-south main line movements. For this service, ten 1,500 volt electric locomotives were built at Darlington to haul 1,000 ton trains: they remained in service for 20 years, but in 1935, with the decline of coal mining in West Durham, the system was abandoned and steam traction restored. Raven also had in mind the electrification of the East Coast main line, but this scheme did not reach fruition.

With the grouping of 1923, H. N. Gresley from the Great Northern Railway was appointed CME of the new company and Raven had to be satisfied with the post of Technical Adviser, which he retained for only a short time. At the grouping, the NER handed over 2,151 steam locomotives (including 138 from the Hull & Barnsley Railway) and 13 electric locomotives.

Bogie coaches were introduced into NER internal services in 1895: for ten years all new stock was fitted with clerestory roofs to the design of David Bain, and even after Bain's departure for the Midland Railway in 1902 the same basic design was followed, and it was not until 1905 that a change was made to elliptical roofs, initially with matchboard sided stock. However, in the following year, new vehicles reverted to panelled sides to the Bain design, and the internal layout was the same as in the clerestory vehicles, the only difference being the new type of roof.

Some stock had internal corridors, but gangway corridor stock was not introduced until 1908, when striking new trains were provided for the Hull – Liverpool and Newcastle – Liverpool services. Most of the gang-way vehicles were carried on eight wheels, but some 65ft 6in dining cars were carried on two six-wheel bogies. The NER also used petrol driven railcars of various sorts on some of its local services, but many of these were worked by steam autocars – a BTP 0-4-4 tank engine with a coach (or coaches) at one (or both) ends, capable of being driven from the coach that was leading, with only the fireman on the footplate.

The North Eastern was a partner, with the Great Northern and the North British, in the provision of a fleet of vehicles to work East Coast services between London and Edinburgh. This tripartite arrangement was made in 1860, with each company financing the scheme in proportion to its share of the East Coast mileage.

Originally, four-wheel and six-wheel vehicles were used, but bogie coaches were used from 1893. At first all the stock was built by the Great Northern at Doncaster, or by contractors, and it was not until 1895 that York turned out the first NER built coach for the ECJS: this was sleeping car 234. Most of the bogie stock ran on eight wheels, but twelve-wheel stock was also used, some vehicles weighing almost 40 tons.

The NER was also part-owner of 36 vehicles used between London and Newcastle, known as Great Northern & North Eastern Joint Stock.

The wagon stock was notable for the number of high-capacity mineral wagons: most of them were 20 ton hopper wagons, and with their high sloping sides they were easily distinguishable. They were used where the modern (1900–1914) colliery screens had been built to take 20 ton wagons: the older screens were restricted to 10 and 12 ton wagons. From the collieries in Northumberland and Durham they were worked to the staiths – long, high wooden gantries on the bank of a river – and when the bottom doors of the wagons were opened, the coal was allowed to gravitate into the holds of the ships tied up alongside. With the decline of the coal industry, many of the staiths had been dismantled, but a few still remain on Tyneside and at Blyth. The small port of Blyth was convenient for one of the largest colliery complexes in the north, that at Ashington, and here 40 ton bogie hopper wagons were used between screens and staiths. Originally these large wagons were fitted with Westinghouse air brakes to speed up the running, but delay caused by coupling and uncoupling outweighed the time saved in running and the air brakes were removed.

Many of the staiths and docks along the north east coast were owned by the North Eastern. At Hull, all but one of the docks had been taken over from the Hull Dock Company in 1893: the other, Alexandra Dock, was built and owned by the Hull & Barnsley Railway, which remained independent until 1922. At Middlesbrough the dock was built privately in 1842, to handle coal coming down from West Durham over the Stockton & Darlington Railway, but it was purchased by the S&DR in 1849 and passed into NER ownership in 1863.

At Hartlepool, a network of docks came from the Hartlepool Dock & Railway and from the West Hartlepool Harbour & Railway, whilst further north, Tyne Dock was another important coal shipping point. Staiths were also provided on the north bank of the Tyne for coal coming down from the pits in southern Northumberland, and also further up-river at Dunston, on the south bank.

At Blyth the accommodation consisted solely of staiths for loading coal into ships in the river. The staiths were on both banks and at one time handled more than six million tons of coal in a year: although the practice of shipping coal at Blyth goes back to Blyth & Tyne Railway days, the extensive development of the shipping facilities was mainly brought about by the NER.

For the dock interests there was a separate Engineer, and to handle the traffic the company employed a large staff of men with grades and posts more suited to water transport than to rail transport. There was also a large fleet of hoppers, barges, tugs, waterboats, floating cranes, grab dredgers, bucket dredgers etc, and the company was also involved in ships sailing to continental ports through the Wilsons & North Eastern Railway Shipping Co. Ltd., and the Hull & Netherlands

Steamship Company Ltd. Although the passenger traffic at Hull was never large, a station at Riverside Quay handled boat trains from various parts of the country.

The North Eastern had some fine stations, the most impressive being Newcastle, now well past its centenary, and York, whose centenary is in 1977. Newcastle has undergone extension, particularly on the south side and at the east end, the former to provide improved through platform accommodation, and the latter to accommodate the local traffic coming in from both banks of the river to the east of the city. The services to the coast on the north bank were electrified in 1904, assisting greatly in the development of Tynemouth, Whitley Bay, and Monkseaton as residential areas, but although electrification of the lines on the south bank was considered by the NER, it was not until 1938 that this was actually accomplished.

At York the accent has always been on main line traffic, but the Leeds – Scarborough service has also been of importance. The fact that York handled trains from the Great Central, Great Eastern, Great Northern, Lancashire & Yorkshire, London & North Western, and Midland companies is well known, and these were normally worked by foreign company's engines. The North Eastern was not afraid of these companies abstracting traffic, but rather the reverse. Ariving at York the intruders brought in passengers from Lancashire, the Midlands, East Anglia, and the south, almost all requiring to go north or east – and the only way they could do so was over the metals of the North Eastern! Similarly, York was a great distribution point: Passengers arriving from the north, or from the east coast, wished to continue their journey to Lancashire, the Midlands, East Anglia, or the south of England, and they could be carried there by the foreign companies. Thus if there was sufficient traffic to keep all the six intruders happy, it meant that the North Eastern was six times happier as the passengers travelled to York by the North Eastern!

Leeds New station, opened in 1869, was owned jointly with the London & North Western, and its main traffic was Hull – Liverpool and Newcastle — Liverpool, with less important trains serving the intermediate stations to east and west. Some of the Newcastle trains ran via Harrogate, and there was also a residential traffic to this Yorkshire spa. The original portion of New station was covered by an impressive Mansard roof, and over the years extensions took place at both ends. The station was built entirely on arches over roads, a river, and a canal! It had no imposing portico, but an unpretentious entrance tucked away in New Station Street.

Hull Paragon was rebuilt over eighty years ago to provide a spacious station, all the platforms being bays as the station is a terminus. However, in recent years the station has been modernised. Darlington has two stations: Bank Top on the main line was built in 1887, replacing an earlier station on the same site. At the time of writing, two old Stockton & Darlington Railway locomotives are preserved on the platform — *Locomotion* of 1825 and *Derwent* of 1845, but both are scheduled to be moved to North Road station, the former Stockton & Darlington station built in 1842, which has been converted into the National Railway Museum opened in 1975.

Many of the smaller stations originally had covered train sheds, notably those on the York & North Midland lines at Market Weighton, Driffield, Beverley, Pocklington, Rillington, Pickering, Church Fenton etc, with further examples at Barnard Castle, Kirkby Stephen, Monkwearmouth, and Tweedmouth. Over the years most of these roofs have been demolished, but a few examples remain in East Yorkshire — or North Humberside, to give it the new administrative area title — particularly at Beverley and Pocklington. At Beverley the roof is still used for its original purpose, to protect the passengers from the weather, but at Pocklington the station was closed in 1965 and it has now been converted into a gymnasium for Pocklington School. Some restoration and repair work, and the provision of end walls, has transformed this old station.

Not many wayside stations are now in railway use, but many of the buildings remain, in use as private residences, garages, pig-farms, county council highways department depots, offices, sawmills, field-study centres etc.

The North Eastern section of the East Coast main line incorporated some notable bridges, the swing bridges over the Ouse at Selby and Naburn; the stone bridge over the Tees near Croft Spa, taking the traveller from Yorkshire into County Durham; the viaducts at Croxdale, Durham, and Chester-le-Street; and the striking entry over the Tyne into Newcastle via the High Level Bridge, or the more modern King Edward Bridge. At the northern extremity of the NER was the Royal Border Bridge spanning the Tweed valley at Berwick: however, the Tweed is not the border between England and Scotland in spite of the title.

Wooden viaducts were not common in the north east, but some examples existed at Ripon, Browney, North Seaton, and Knitsley etc, and also on the Waterhouses branch. Most were rebuilt in metal, but that at Knitsley (on the Lanchester Valley branch) was buried to become an embankment, and one at Ushaw Moor (on the Waterhouses branch) lasted until the 1960s. The stone viaduct at Kilton (near Loftus) was another to become an embankment when its foundations became undermined.

The most notable viaducts were, however, on the line from Barnard Castle to Kirkby Stephen and Tebay, opened by the South Durham & Lancashire Union Railway in 1861. These were of three types, all stone, all metal, or a combination of the two, and they were all designed by Thomas Bouch, who later designed the ill-fated Tay Bridge, which collapsed into the river during a storm in 1879. Economic considerations have led to the complete demolition of the metal viaducts for their scrap value, notably Belah and Deepdale, but with the combined viaducts, only the metal has been recovered, leaving the piers standing as a memorial to a fascinating line. However, all the stone viaducts have remained virtually untouched, although if the demand for stone houses increases it may become economically viable to demolish the stone viaducts also!

March 1975   Ken Hoole

Constituent Companies of the North Eastern Railway with details of the principal Acts of Parliament

North Eastern Railway		by Act	date
formed with change of name		17/18 Vic cap 211	31-7-54
from amalgamation of:			
YORK & NORTH MIDLAND RLY	inc	6 Wm IV cap 81	21-6-36
LEEDS NORTHERN RLY			
change of name		14/15 Vic cap 47	3-7-51
from			
LEEDS & THIRSK RLY	inc	8/9 Vic cap 104	21-7-45
both Y&NM and LN dissolved by NER formation Act, and vested in YN&B			
YORK, NEWCASTLE & BERWICK RLY			
change of name		10/11 Vic cap 133	9-7-47
from amalgamation of:			
YORK & NEWCASTLE RLY			
change of name		9/10 Vic cap 330	3-8-46
from			
NEWCASTLE & DARLINGTON JUNCTION RLY	inc	5 Vic cap 80	18-6-42
NEWCASTLE & BERWICK RLY	inc	8/9 Vic cap 163	31-7-45
MALTON & DRIFFIELD JUNCTION RLY	inc	9/10 Vic cap 77	26-6-46
the NER Act contained provisions for the M&DJ to be included in the amalgamation if effected within 3 months of its passing: completed 28-10-54			

Amalgamations effected by Constituent Companies

YORK & NORTH MIDLAND RLY:			
EAST & WEST YORKSHIRE JUNCTION RLY	inc	9/10 Vic cap 164	16-7-46
amalgamated with Y&NM		15 Vic cap 57	28-5-52
HULL & SELBY RLY	inc	6 Wm IV cap 80	21-6-36
leased to Y&NM		9/10 Vic cap 241	27-7-46
(ratification of agreement in force from 1-7-45)			
sold to NER 1872 under leasing Act			
LEEDS & SELBY RLY	inc	11 Geo IV cap 59	29-5-30
sold to Y&NM		7 Vic cap 21	23-5-44
WHITBY & PICKERING RLY	inc	3 Wm IV cap 35	6-5-33
sold to Y&NM		8/9 Vic cap 57	30-6-45
YORK, NEWCASTLE & BERWICK RLY:			
GREAT NORTH OF ENGLAND, CLARENCE &			
HARTLEPOOL JUNCTION RLY	inc	1 Vic cap 95	3-7-37
leased in perpetuity to YN&B		11/12 Vic cap 82	22-7-48
HARTLEPOOL DOCK & RLY	inc	2 Wm IV cap 67	1-6-32
leased to YN&B		11/12 Vic cap 81	22-7-48
amalgamated with NER		20/21 Vic cap 33	13-7-57
YORK & NEWCASTLE RLY:			
DURHAM & SUNDERLAND RLY	inc	4/5 Wm IV cap 96	13-8-34
purchased by Y&N (from 1-1-47)		9/10 Vic cap 235	27-7-46

–(as Newcastle & Darlington Junction Rly):

BRANDLING JUNCTION RLY	inc	6 Wm IV cap 57	7-6-36
following private purchase of land by J & R W			
Brandling		5/6 Wm IV cap 83	21-7-35
(Act not used for acquisition of land – acquired under			
wayleaves)			
purchased by N&DJ		8/9 Vic cap 92	21-7-45
DURHAM JUNCTION RLY	inc	4 Wm IV cap 57	16-6-34
sold to N&DJ		7 Vic cap 27	23-5-44
GREAT NORTH OF ENGLAND RLY	inc	6/7 Wm IV cap 105	4-7-36
leased and sold to N&DJ		9/10 Vic cap 242	27-7-46
WEARMOUTH DOCK	Inc by	Royal Letters Patent	26-7-35
sold to N&DJ		9/10 Vic cap 235	27-7-46
PONTOP & SOUTH SHIELDS RLY	inc	5 Vic cap 27	13-5-42
incorporation included transfer of eastern portion of:			
STANHOPE & TYNE RLY		no Act	
built under wayleaves		Deed of Settlement	3-2-34
Co wound up 5-2-41 (western portion from the foot			
of Carr House East Incline sold to Derwent Iron Co: see			
WEAR & DERWENT RLY below and section notes)			
P&SS sold to N&DJ		9/10 Vic cap 330	3-8-46
NEWCASTLE & BERWICK RLY:			
NEWCASTLE & NORTH SHIELDS RLY	inc	6 Wm IV cap 76	21-6-36
sold to N&B		8/9 Vic cap 163	31-7-45

North Eastern Railway Amalgamations

STOCKTON & DARLINGTON RAILWAY	inc	1/2 Geo IV cap 44	19-4-21
amalgamated with NER		26/27 Vic cap 122	13-7-63
Stockton & Darlington Rly amalgamations:			
DARLINGTON & BARNARD CASTLE RLY	inc	17/18 Vic cap 115	3-7-54
amalgamated with S&D		21/22 Vic cap 116	23-7-58
EDEN VALLEY RLY	inc	21 Vic cap 14	21-5-58
amalgamated with S&D		25/26 Vic cap 106	30-6-62
FROSTERLEY & STANHOPE RLY	inc	24/25 Vic cap 72	28-6-61
transferred to S&D		25/26 Vic cap 106	30-6-62
MIDDLESBROUGH & GUISBROUGH RLY	inc	15 Vic cap 73	17-6-52
amalgamated with S&D		21/22 Vic cap 116	23-7-58
SOUTH DURHAM & LANCASHIRE UNION RLY	inc	20/21 Vic cap 40	13-7-57
amalgamated with S&D		25/26 Vic cap 106	30-6-62
MIDDLESBROUGH & REDCAR RLY	inc	8/9 Vic cap 127	21-7-45
amalgamated with S&D		21/22 Vic cap 116	23-7-58
WEAR VALLEY RLY	inc	8/9 Vic cap 152	31-7-45
amalgamated with S&D		21/22 Vic cap 116	23-7-58
BISHOP AUCKLAND & WEARDALE RLY	inc	1 Vic cap 122	15-7-37
sold to Wear Valley Rly		10/11 Vic cap 292	22-7-47
SHILDON TUNNEL		no Act	
built privately by Shildon Tunnel Co and sold to Wear			
Valley Rly		10/11 Vic cap 292	22-7-47
WEARDALE EXTENSION RLY		no Act	
a project of the Derwent Iron Co but built by S&D – to			
private owners 1845.			
sold to Wear Valley Rly		10/11 Vic cap 292	22-7-47
WEAR & DERWENT RLY(unofficial name)		no Act	
western portion of Stanhope & Tyne – taken over by			
Derwent Iron Co 1841			
leased to S&D 1-1-45			
sold to Wear Valley Rly		10/11 Vic cap 292	22-7-47
latter two became unofficially known as Wear &			
Derwent Junction Rly			

MIDDLESBROUGH DOCK		no Act	
vested in S&D		12/13 Vic cap 54	13-7-49
BEDALE & LEYBURN RLY	inc	16/17 Vic cap 137	4-8-53
vested in NER		22/23 Vic cap 91	8-8-59
NEWCASTLE & CARLISLE RLY	inc	10 Geo IV cap 72	22-5-29
amalgamated with NER		25/26 Vic cap 145	17-7-62
BLAYDON, GATESHEAD & HEBBURN RLY	inc	4 Wm IV cap 26	22-5-34

powers for N&C to construct part of line.
No works commenced when powers taken over by N&C by
mutual consent.

BLYTH & TYNE RLY	inc	15/16 Vic cap 122	30-6-52

(Act of Incorporation involving several early waggonways –
see section notes)

vested in NER		37/38 Vic cap 192	7-8-74
CLEVELAND RLY	inc	21/22 Vic cap 114	23-7-58
amalgamated with NER		28/29 Vic cap 180	5-7-65
DEARNESS VALLEY RLY	inc	18/19 Vic cap 180	30-7-55
sold to NER		20/21 Vic cap 46	13-7-57
HEXHAM & ALLENDALE RLY	inc	28 Vic cap 87	19-6-65
Co dissolved and vested in NER		39/40 Vic cap 102	13-7-76
HULL & HOLDERNESS RLY	inc	16/17 Vic cap 93	8-7-53
Co dissolved and vested in NER		25/26 Vic cap 120	7-7-62
HULL & HORNSEA RLY	inc	25/26 Vic cap 100	30-6-62
amalgamated with NER		29/30 Vic cap 187	16-7-66
HYLTON, SOUTHWICK & MONKWEARMOUTH RLY	inc	34 Vic cap 13	25-5-71
vested in NER		46/47 Vic cap 63	29-6-83
LEEDS, CASTLEFORD & PONTEFRACT JUNCTION RLY	inc	36/37 Vic cap 176	21-7-73
vested in NER		39/40 Vic cap 102	13-7-76
MERRYBENT & DARLINGTON RLY	inc	29 Vic cap 75	11-6-66

powers conferred included provision for purchase by any
company authorised by the Act.

Co wound up		41 Vic cap 93	17-6-78

NER acquired property from Darlington District Bank in 1890
under terms of Act of Incorporation.

vested in NER		63/64 Vic cap 163	30-7-00
SCARBOROUGH, BRIDLINGTON & WEST RIDING JUNCTION RLY	inc	48/49 Vic cap 181	6-8-85
vested in NER retrospective to 1-7-14		4/5 Geo V cap 95	31-7-14
SCARBOROUGH & WHITBY RLY	inc	34/35 Vic cap 85	29-6-71
vested in NER retrospective to 1-7-98		61/62 Vic cap 197	2-8-98
SCOTSWOOD, NEWBURN & WYLAM RLY			
change of name		39 Vic cap 7	7-4-76
from			
SCOTSWOOD, NEWBURN & WYLAM RLY & DOCK	inc	34 Vic cap 48	16-6-71
vested in NER		46/47 Vic cap 63	29-6-83
TEES VALLEY RLY	inc	28 Vic cap 91	19-6-65
vested in NER		45 Vic cap 50	19-6-82
WEAR VALLEY EXTENSION RLY	inc	55/56 Vic cap 128	20-6-92
transfer of powers to NER before completion		57/58 Vic cap 153	31-7-94
WEST DURHAM RLY	inc	2/3 Vic cap 71	4-7-39
(built under wayleaves)			
vested in NER		33/34 Vic cap 105	4-7-70
WHITBY, REDCAR & MIDDLESBROUGH UNION RLY	inc	29/30 Vic cap 195	16-7-66
leased to NER		38/39 Vic cap 156	19-7-75
amalgamated with NER		52/53 Vic cap 60	5-7-89

LONDONDERRY RLY	inc	26 Vic cap 66	8-6-63

private railway authorised for the Marquis of Londonderry to regulate and manage railways between Seaham and Sunderland.

vested in NER(worked by NER from 6-10-00)		63/64 Vic cap 163	30-7-00
WEST HARTLEPOOL HARBOUR & RLY	inc	15/16 Vic cap 142	30-6-52

formed by amalgamation and change of name (effective from 17-5-53) from

HARTLEPOOL WEST HARBOUR & DOCK	inc	7 Vic cap 28	23-5-44
STOCKTON & HARTLEPOOL RLY	inc	5/6 Vic cap 90	30-6-42

      formerly a joint stock company built under a Deed of

Settlement			12-3-39
CLARENCE RLY	inc	9 Geo IV cap 61	23-5-28
leased to S&H		6/7 Vic cap 46	27-6-43

      (leased from 1-9-44 for 21 years – leased in
      perpetuity 1-1-51)

purchased by WHH&R (from 9-4-53)		15/16 Vic cap 142	30-6-52
HULL DOCK	inc	14 Geo III cap 56	20-5-1774
amalgamated with NER retrospective to 1-7-93		56/57 Vic cap 198	24-8-93
NORTH YORKSHIRE & CLEVELAND RLY	inc	17/18 Vic cap 151	10-7-54

property of Co vested in NER (included construction of Rosedale branch)

		22/23 Vic cap 91	8-8-59

Independent Concern

TEES CONSERVANCY			
construction of railway by NER		8 Ed VII cap 34	10-8-08

Independent Company worked by NER

FORCETT RLY	inc	28 Vic cap 61	2-6-65
worked by NER from opening			

Joint Railways

Leeds & Thirsk(NER) / Leeds, Dewsbury & Manchester(LNWR) / Lancashire & Yorkshire / Great Northern:

LEEDS CENTRAL RAILWAY STATION			
joint powers to build station		11/12 Vic cap 71	22-7-48

North Eastern / London & North Western:

LEEDS NEW STATION			
powers to construct station and connections		28/29 Vic cap 267	5-7-65

North Eastern / Lancashire & Yorkshire / Midland / Great Northern / Great Central:

SOUTH YORKSHIRE JOINT LINE COMMITTEE			
NER line authorised		2 Ed VII cap 168	31-7-02
powers transferred to Joint Committee		3 Ed VII cap 253	14-8-03

Lancashire & Yorkshire / West Yorkshire(GNR) / North Eastern:

WEST YORKSHIRE RLY (Methley Joint Rly)	inc	26/27 Vic cap 167	21-7-63
powers transferred to Joint Committee		27/28 Vic cap 60	23-6-64

North Eastern / Midland:

OTLEY & ILKLEY JOINT LINE COMMITTEE			
powers transferred to Joint Committee		24/25 Vic cap 141	11-7-61
MIDLAND & NORTH EASTERN RAILWAY COMPANIES			
COMMITTEE (Swinton & Knottingley Joint Rly)	inc	37/38 Vic cap 133	16-7-74

North Eastern / Hull, Barnsley & West Riding Junction:

certain NER works transferred to Joint Committee		3/4 Geo V cap 47	15-8-13

Joint Powers

North Eastern / North British / Midland / Great Northern

FORTH BRIDGE RLY CO	inc	36/37 Vic cap 237	5-8-73
further powers of Co and partners	re-inc	45/46 Vic cap 114	12-7-82

Light Railways

CAWOOD, WISTOW & SELBY LIGHT RLY	inc	59/60 Vic cap 46	2-7-96
purchased by NER		63/64 Vic cap 163	3-7-00
BRACKENHILL LIGHT RLY		Light Railway Order	19-3-01
worked by NER from opening under powers of NER Act		1/2 Geo V cap 94	18-8-11
GOOLE & MARSHLAND LIGHT RLY (Marshland Jcn – Fockerby)		Light Railway Order	16-8-98
ISLE OF AXHOLME LIGHT RLY (Reedness Jcn – Haxey Jcn)		Light Railway Order	11-3-99
both dissolved and vested jointly in NER and L&YR under powers of NER Act with title – Axholme Joint Rly Committee		2 Ed VII cap 168	31-7-02

Amalgamation of North Eastern Rly and Hull, Barnsley & West Riding Junction Rly & Dock by Statutory Rules and Orders 1922 No 393, operative from 1-4-22.

Notes:

1. DERWENT IRON CO:

This company was set up in Conside (now Consett) c1840 and was heavily dependent on limestone from the Weardale quarries at Stanhope. When the S&T was wound up after having problems with the high cost of wayleaves, the eastern portion from the foot of Carr House East Incline was taken over under an Act by a new company, the Pontop & South Shields Rly., and the western end from thence to Stanhope by the Derwent Iron Co, when it became known unofficially as the Wear & Derwent Rly. The construction by the S&D of the line from Crook to Waskerley (a Derwent Iron Co project) by a subsidiary company, the Weardale Extension Rly, included provisions for the lease of the western end of the Derwent company's line to the S&D. This was completed early in 1845.

The company suffered heavily after the collapse of the Northumberland & Durham Bank in 1857, and after a period of management by a subsidiary company set up by the NER and the S&D, during which it became the Derwent & Consett Iron Co in 1858, it finally became the Consett Iron Co in 1864.

2. SEGHILL RLY:

Towards the end of the 1830s, the owners of Seghill Colliery were becoming dissatisfied with the services to Tyneside by the Cramlington Waggonway, and decided to build their own line to Percy Main east of and almost adjacent to the Cramlington line. This line, together with an earlier waggonway to Seaton Delaval Colliery, and a continuation to Hartley New Winning Colliery, became the nucleus of the Blyth & Tyne Rly. In 1845, the building of an extension was begun, known as the Blyth & Tyne Jcn. Rly., from Hartley towards Blyth. This was undertaken by the lessees of Cowpen and Hartley collieries, and was to join their waggonway to Cowpen Colliery, south-west of Blyth.

By 1846, when the new line was opened, these lines had become a private railway under the unofficial title Blyth, Seghill & Percy Main Rly – shortened in 1847 to Blyth & Tyne. Following the opening of a private line to Bedlington Colliery in 1850, an Act was applied for in 1852 to incorporate the various lines forming the Blyth & Tyne as a public company, due mainly to the refusal by the Board of Inland Revenue to grant an exemption of Passenger Duty to a private company. Part of the line to Bedlington was relaid a few years later to become a section of the branch to Morpeth.

Lines for which no authenticated dates have been traced

Abbreviation: RJD – Airey's or Railway Clearing House Junction Diagram Books.

Whilst both the maps and diagram books of Airey, and the RCH, are a useful source of reference, they cannot be termed a reliable guide to line opening periods. Where an accurate date has been found, even dated editions have been found to be incorrect.

NE12: Line to Frickley Colliery.
Colliery sunk about 1905, and it is thought likely that the NER connection was opened contemporaneously with the H&B one in 1907.

NE15: Line to original cattle dock at Newcastle, Forth, station.
Possibly opened 1847, at the same time as, or shortly after, the main line to Forth station.

NE16: South Shields – St. Bedes Jcn to Tyne Dock Bottom Jcn.
Opened c1885 – no information. This line was an inter-connection between two sidings to St.Bedes chemical works, one from Tyne Dock, and one from St.Bedes Jcn.

NE16: South Shields – S&T to BJR connection at Harton Jcn.
A direct connection was authorised by Acts of 1865 and 1876. The presence of the second Act makes it likely that the connection was opened 2-6-79. It also seems likely that the severance of the S&T line at Garden Lane Jcn was carried out around this date.

NE17b: S&T – diversion to bypass Parkhead wheel.
No information other than being carried out about 1847.

NE17b: Branch to South Medomsley Colliery.
Agreement is known to have existed between colliery owners and NER dated 1862. Not known if an earlier agreement existed. Line opened privately.

NE18a: Durham – Broomside Jcn to Sherburn Colliery Jcn.
No definite date known. Shown as opened in 1859 in the official List of Lines published by the LNER. Map evidence points to around the same date, but no confirmation.

NE19a: Hartlepool – northern line around Central/Union Dock complex.
Appears to have been a through line, probably via sidings, by 1894, but had become a through running line by 1914.

NE19a: Hartlepool – Burn Road Goods.
No information – probably opened prior to 1865, but in use only as a siding until a depot was built at some date after 1895.

NE19a: Hartlepool – Cliff House Branch.
No information – originally sidings to ironworks from north and south. Probably opened through prior to 1865.

NE19b: Ferryhill – eastern connection to Tursdale Colliery.
No information – this line is of uncertain ownership, but appears to have been in the possession of the NER at about the turn of the century, being either built by them, or leased to them from the colliery company. How long it remained in their possession is at present unknown.

NE20a: Shildon – S&D line to Adelaide Colliery.
No information – thought to have been opened about 1842.

NE20a: Shildon – spur to west from Black Boy Branch.
No information, but thought to have been opened about 1850.

NE20b: Darlington – east to north connection at S&D crossing.
Used c1861 for ironstone traffic to Ferryhill, but possibly in use earlier.

NE23a: Leeds – line to Monkbridge Ironworks.
Thought to have been opened about 1854, but the line does not appear in the RJD until diagram dated 1913.

NE24: Hull – branch to Foreign Cattle Depot.
No information – map evidence points to the line being opened between c1855 and 1884.

NE24: Hull – Sculcoates/Stepney Goods Branches.
No information – opened by 1884/5, but is thought to have been opened much earlier.

NE24: Hull – Albert Dock Goods Branch.
No information – opened by Hull Dock Co. Dock opened 1869, with line probably being opened about 1871/2.

NE24: Hull – St. Andrews Dock Branch to north side of Dock.
No information – dock opened by Hull Dock Co. 1883. Line open by 1884/5.

NE24: Hull – St. Andrews Dock Branch to south side of Dock.
No information – line opened between 1884 and 1910.

NE24: Hull – NE/H&B connection from Albert Dock West Junction.
No information – the connection does not appear on the 1910 Ordnance Survey, but is shown on the RJD dated 1915.

NE24: Hull – Wilmington Goods Branch.
No information – opened by 1884, but is thought to have been opened much earlier.

NE24: Hull – Creek Goods Line.
No information – map evidence points to the line being opened between c1855 and 1884.

NE24: Hull – Dansom Lane Depot.
No information – opened between 1904 and c1910.

NE24: Hull – Drypool Goods.
No information – opened about 1904, when it first appeared separately in the RCH Handbook. The original line to Victoria Dock was cut here when the branch was re-aligned to bypass the level crossing at Hedon Rd. c1905.

THE MAPS

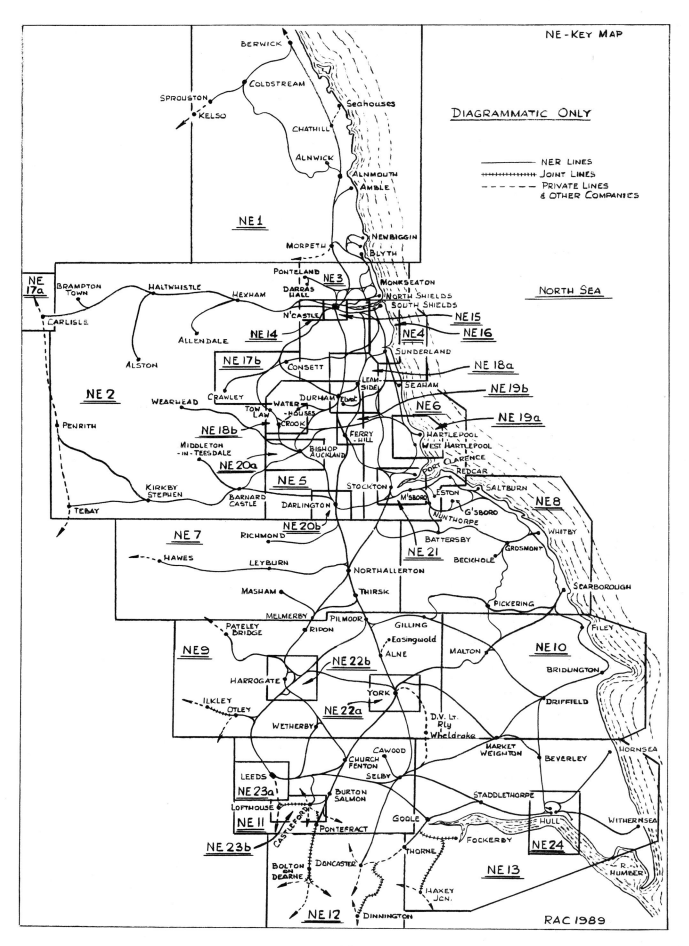

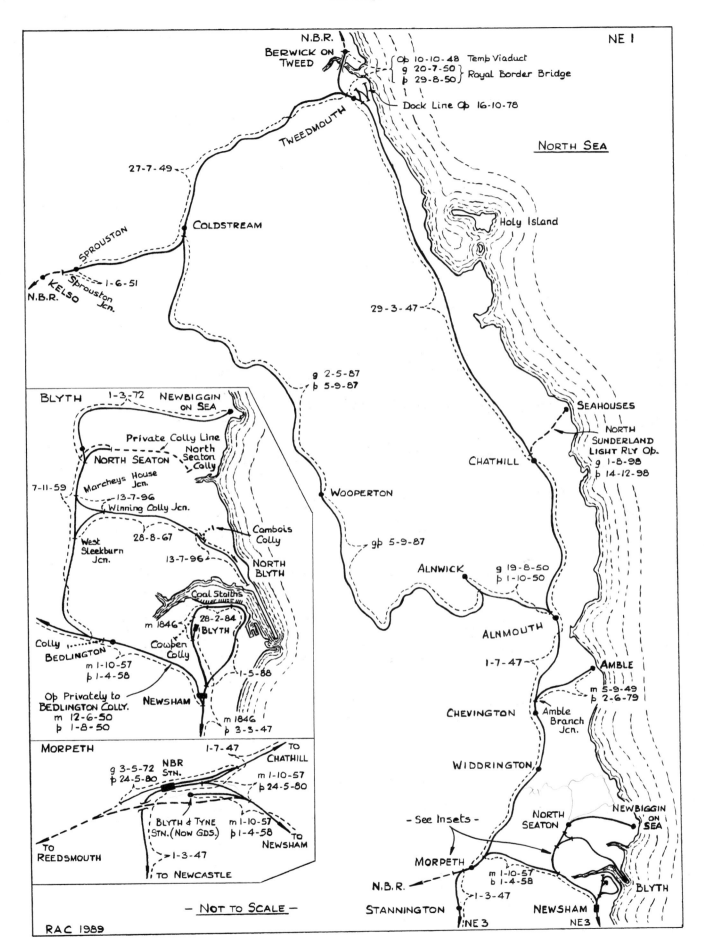

NE 1

N.B.R.
BERWICK ON TWEED

Op 10-10-48 Temp Viaduct
g 20-7-50 } Royal Border Bridge
þ 29-8-50 }

TWEEDMOUTH

Dock Line Op 16-10-78

NORTH SEA

27-7-49

COLDSTREAM

Holy Island

SPROUSTON

1-6-51

KELSO
N.B.R.

Sprouston Jcn.

29-3-47

g 2-5-87
þ 5-9-87

SEAHOUSES

NORTH SUNDERLAND LIGHT RLY Op.
g 1-8-98
þ 14-12-98

CHATHILL

WOOPERTON

gþ 5-9-87

ALNWICK

g 19-8-50
þ 1-10-50

ALNMOUTH

1-7-47

AMBLE
m 5-9-49
þ 2-6-79

CHEVINGTON

Amble Branch Jcn.

WIDDRINGTON

- See Insets -

NORTH SEATON

NEWBIGGIN ON SEA

MORPETH

N.B.R.

m 1-10-57
þ 1-4-58

BLYTH

STANNINGTON

1-3-47

NEWSHAM

NE 3   NE 3

Inset: BLYTH

BLYTH   1-3-72 NEWBIGGIN ON SEA

Private Colly Line
North Seaton Colly

NORTH SEATON

Marcheys House Jcn.

7-11-59

13-7-96

Winning Colly Jcn.

Cambois Colly

28-8-67

NORTH BLYTH

West Sleekburn Jcn.

13-7-96

Coal Staiths

Colly
BEDLINGTON

m 1846

28-2-84

BLYTH

m 1-10-57
þ 1-4-58

Cowpen Colly

Op Privately to BEDLINGTON COLLY.
m 12-6-50
þ 1-8-50

NEWSHAM

1-5-88

m 1846
þ 3-3-47

Inset: MORPETH

MORPETH

1-7-47 TO CHATHILL

g 3-5-72
þ 24-5-80

NBR STN.

m 1-10-57
þ 24-5-80

Blyth & Tyne STN. (Now GDS.)

m 1-10-57
þ 1-4-58

TO NEWSHAM

TO REEDSMOUTH

1-3-47

TO NEWCASTLE

— NOT TO SCALE —

RAC 1989

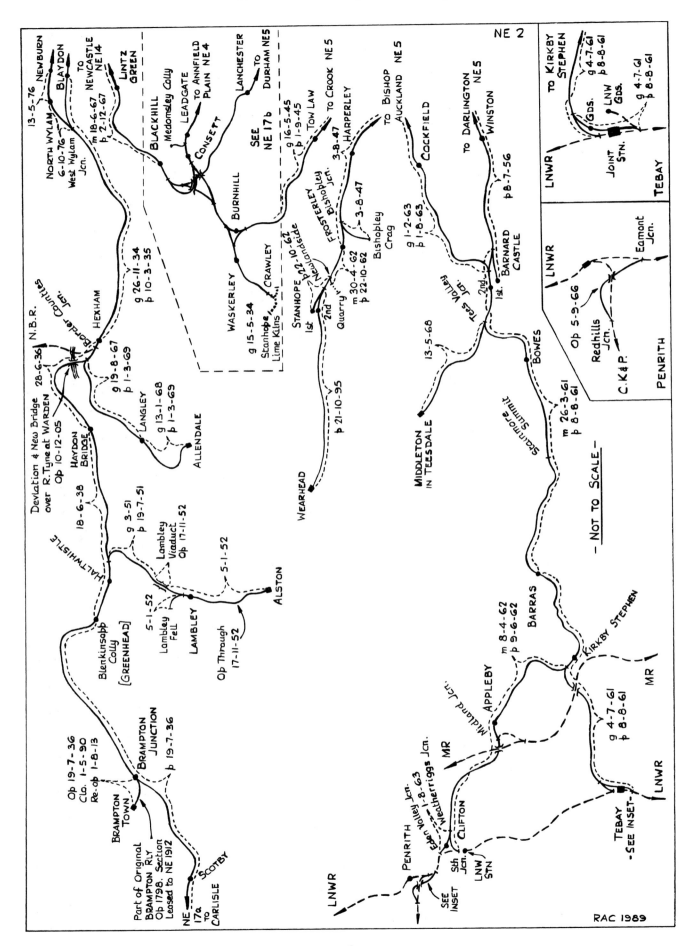

NE 2

RAC 1989

- NOT TO SCALE -

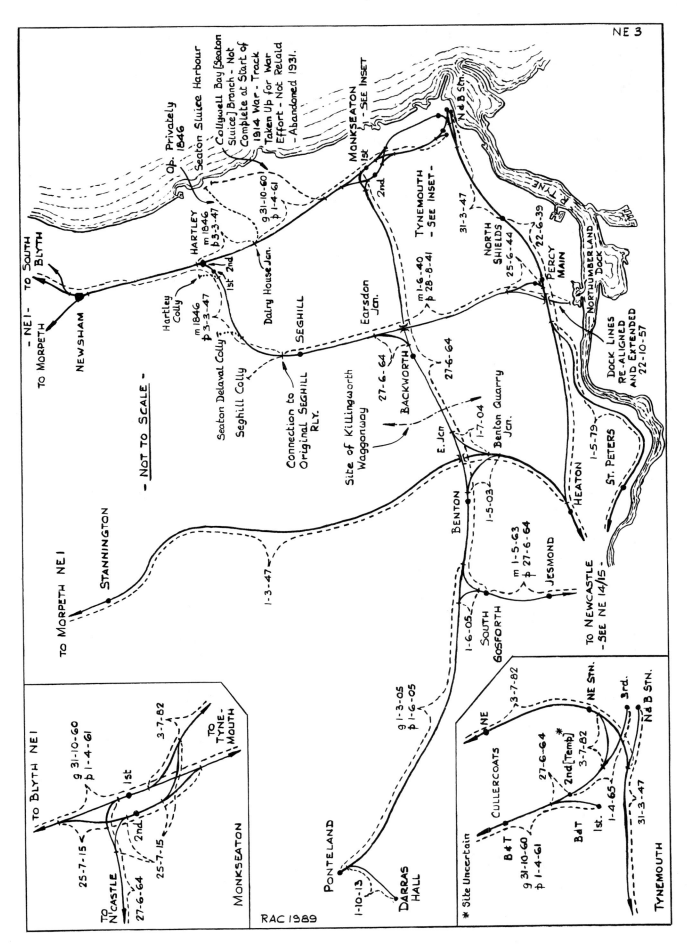

RAC 1989

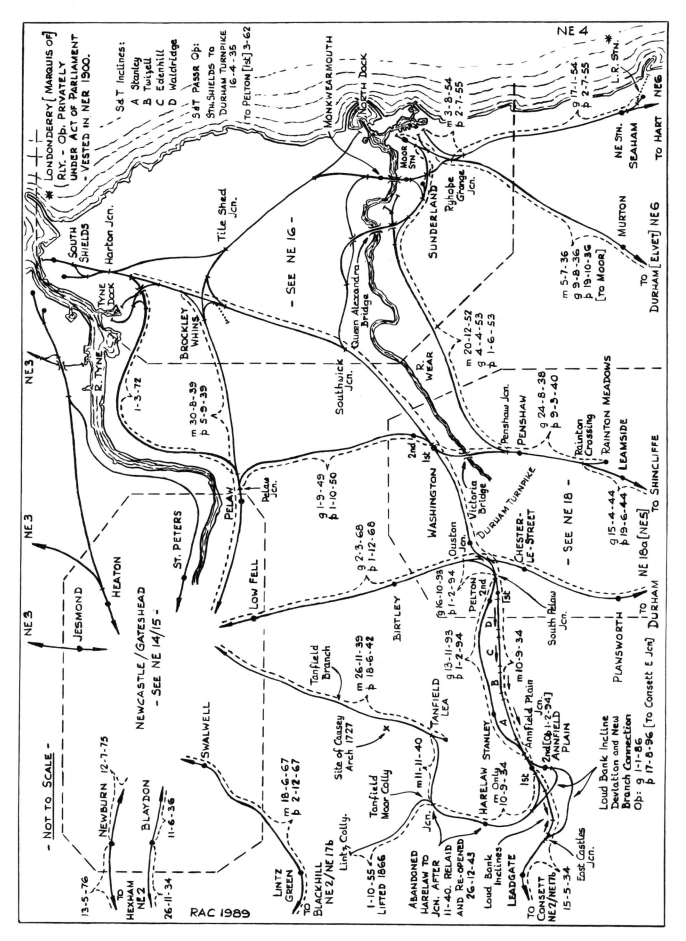

NE 4

- NOT TO SCALE -

LONDONDERRY [MARQUIS OF] RLY. - Op. PRIVATELY UNDER ACT OF PARLIAMENT - VESTED IN NER 1900.

S&T Inclines:
A Stanley
B Twizell
C Edenhill
D Waldridge

S&T PASSR Op:
Sth. SHIELDS to DURHAM TURNPIKE 16-4-35
To PELTON [1st] 3-62

RAC 1989

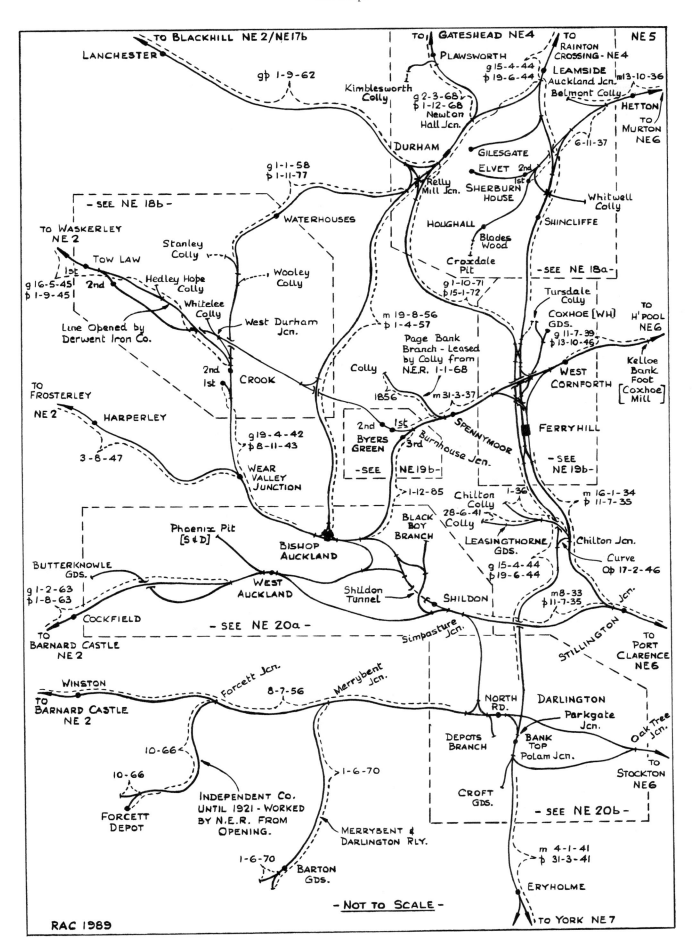

TO BLACKHILL NE 2/NE17b
TO GATESHEAD NE 4
TO RAINTON CROSSING - NE 4
NE 5

LANCHESTER

PLAWSWORTH
g 15-4-44
þ 19-6-44

LEAMSIDE
Auckland Jcn.
m 13-10-36

gþ 1-9-62

Kimblesworth
Colly

Belmont Colly

HETTON

TO MURTON NE 6

g 2-3-68
þ 1-12-68
Newton
Hall Jcn.

DURHAM

GILESGATE

ELVET 2nd
1st

6-11-37

g 1-1-58
þ 1-11-77

Relly
Mill Jcn.

SHERBURN
HOUSE

WHITWELL
COLLY

- SEE NE 18b -

WATERHOUSES

HOUGHALL

SHINCLIFFE

TO WASKERLEY
NE 2

Stanley
Colly

Blades
Wood

- SEE NE 18a -

Tow Law 1st

Hedley Hope
Colly

Wooley
Colly

Croxdale
Pit

Tursdale
Colly

TO H'POOL
NE 6

g 16-5-45
þ 1-9-45

2nd

Whitelee
Colly

g 1-10-71
þ 15-1-72

COXHOE [WH]
GDS.
g 11-7-39
þ 13-10-46

West Durham
Jcn.

m 19-8-56
þ 1-4-57

Kelloe
Bank
Foot
[Coxhoe]
Mill

Line Opened by
Derwent Iron Co.

2nd
1st CROOK

Colly

Page Bank
Branch - Leased
by Colly from
N.E.R. 1-1-68

1856

WEST
CORNFORTH

TO
FROSTERLEY
NE 2

HARPERLEY

m 31-3-37

FERRYHILL

3-8-47

g 19-4-42
þ 8-11-43

2nd
BYERS
GREEN
3rd
1st

SPENNYMOOR

Burnhouse Jcn.

- SEE
NE19b -

- SEE NE19b -

WEAR
VALLEY
JUNCTION

>1-12-85

Chilton
Colly

1-36

m 16-1-34
þ 11-7-35

Phoenix Pit
[S&D]

BLACK
BOY
BRANCH

28-6-41
Colly

LEASINGTHORNE
GDS.

Chilton Jcn.

Curve
Op 17-2-46

BISHOP
AUCKLAND

g 15-4-44
þ 19-6-44

BUTTERKNOWLE
GDS.

WEST
AUCKLAND

Shildon
Tunnel

SHILDON

m8-33
þ 11-7-35

Jcn.

g 1-2-63
þ 1-8-63

STILLINGTON

TO PORT
CLARENCE
NE 6

COCKFIELD

- SEE NE 20a -

Simpasture
Jcn.

TO
BARNARD CASTLE
NE 2

Forcett Jcn.

Merrybent
Jcn.

WINSTON

8-7-56

DARLINGTON

Oak Tree
Jcn.

TO
BARNARD CASTLE
NE 2

NORTH
RD.

Parkgate
Jcn.

10-66

DEPOTS
BRANCH

BANK
TOP
Polam Jcn.

TO
STOCKTON
NE 6

10-66

>1-6-70

FORCETT
DEPOT

INDEPENDENT CO.
UNTIL 1921 - WORKED
BY N.E.R. FROM
OPENING.

MERRYBENT &
DARLINGTON RLY.

CROFT
GDS.

- SEE NE 20b -

1-6-70

BARTON
GDS.

m 4-1-41
þ 31-3-41

ERYHOLME

- NOT TO SCALE -

TO YORK NE 7

RAC 1989

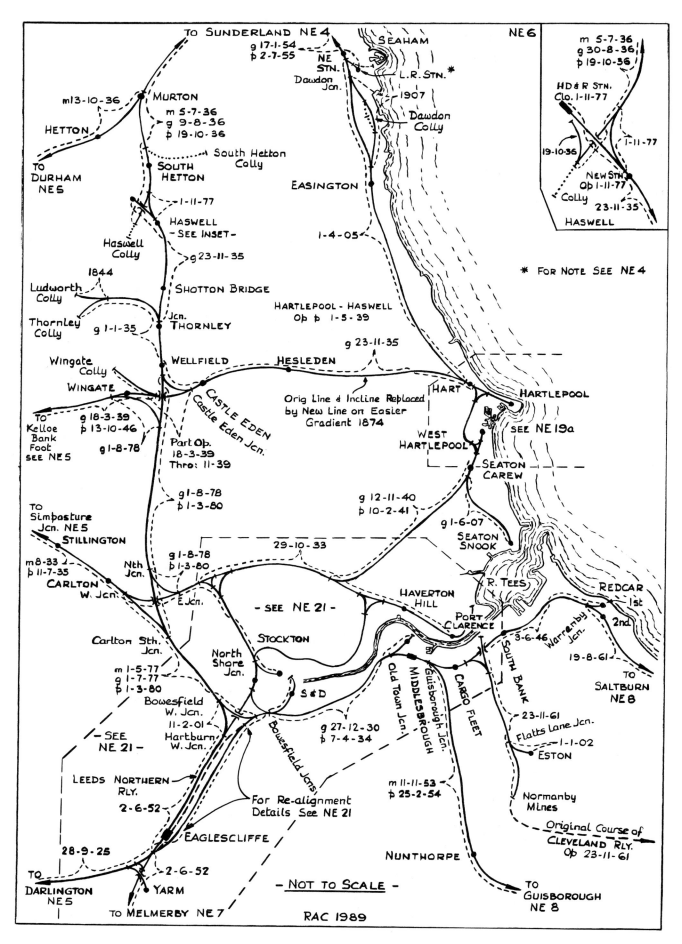

NE 6

TO SUNDERLAND NE 4
g 17-1-54
p 2-7-55

SEAHAM

NE STN.
Dawdon Jcn.
L.R. STN. *
1907
Dawdon Colly

m 5-7-36
g 30-8-36
p 19-10-36

HD&R STN.
Clo. 1-11-77

19-10-36
1-11-77

NEW STN.
Op 1-11-77

Colly

23-11-35

HASWELL

* FOR NOTE SEE NE 4

m13-10-36
MURTON
m 5-7-36
g 9-8-36
p 19-10-36
HETTON

South Hetton Colly

SOUTH HETTON

EASINGTON

TO DURHAM NE5

-1-11-77

HASWELL
– SEE INSET –

Haswell Colly

1-4-05

g 23-11-35

1844

Ludworth Colly

SHOTTON BRIDGE

HARTLEPOOL - HASWELL
Op p 1-5-39

Thornley Colly

g 1-1-35

Jcn. THORNLEY

g 23-11-35

Wingate Colly

WELLFIELD

HESLEDEN

WINGATE

CASTLE EDEN
Castle Eden Jcn.

HART

HARTLEPOOL

Orig Line & Incline Replaced
by New Line on Easier
Gradient 1874

SEE NE 19a

TO Kelloe Bank Foot
SEE NE5

g 18-3-39
p 13-10-46

g 1-8-78

WEST HARTLEPOOL

Part Op.
18-3-39
Thro: 11-39

SEATON CAREW

TO Simposture Jcn. NE 5

g 1-8-78
p 1-3-80

g 12-11-40
p 10-2-41

STILLINGTON

g 1-6-07

SEATON SNOOK

m8-33
p 11-7-35

29-10-33

R. TEES

REDCAR

CARLTON
W. Jcn.

g 1-8-78
p 1-3-80

Nth Jcn.

HAVERTON HILL

1st

E Jcn.

PORT CLARENCE

3-6-46

Warrenby Jcn.

2nd

Carlton Sth. Jcn.

– SEE NE 21 –

STOCKTON

SOUTH BANK

CARGO FLEET

19-8-61

North Shore Jcn.

TO SALTBURN NE 8

m 1-5-77
g 1-7-77
p 1-3-80

S&D

Old Town Jcn.

Guisborough Jcn.

MIDDLESBROUGH

23-11-61

Flatts Lane Jcn.

Bowesfield W. Jcn.

Bowesfield Jcns.

1-1-02

11-2-01

g 27-12-30
p 7-4-34

ESTON

– SEE NE 21 –

Hartburn W. Jcn.

For Re-alignment
Details See NE 21

m 11-11-53
p 25-2-54

Normanby Mines

LEEDS NORTHERN RLY.

2-6-52

Original Course of CLEVELAND RLY.
Op 23-11-61

28-9-25

EAGLESCLIFFE

NUNTHORPE

2-6-52

– NOT TO SCALE –

TO DARLINGTON NE5

YARM

TO GUISBOROUGH NE 8

TO MELMERBY NE 7

RAC 1989

30

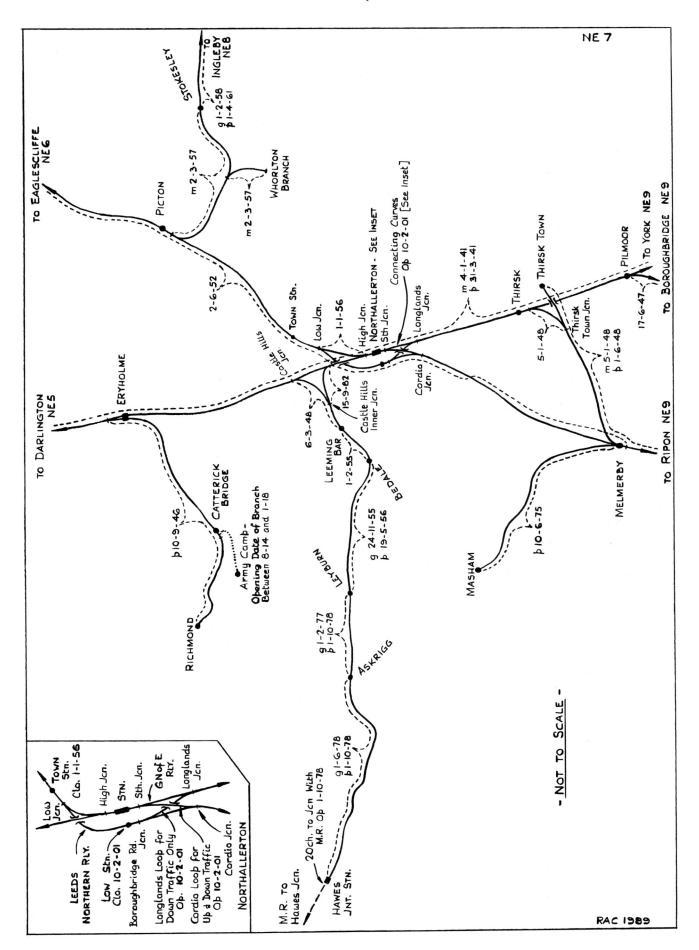

RAC 1989

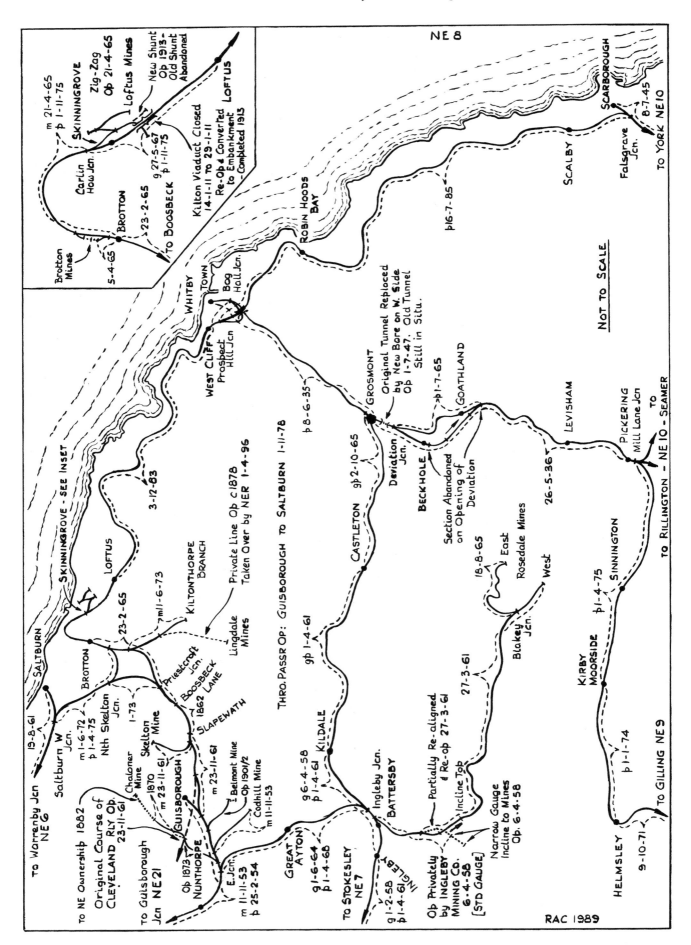

NE 8

Not to Scale

RAC 1989

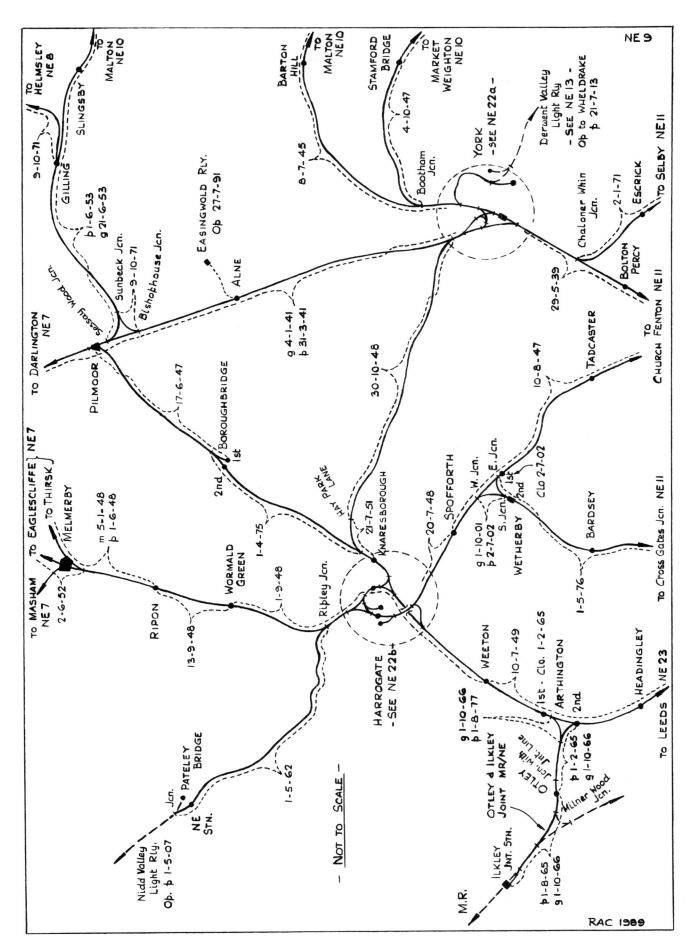

NE 9

RAC 1989

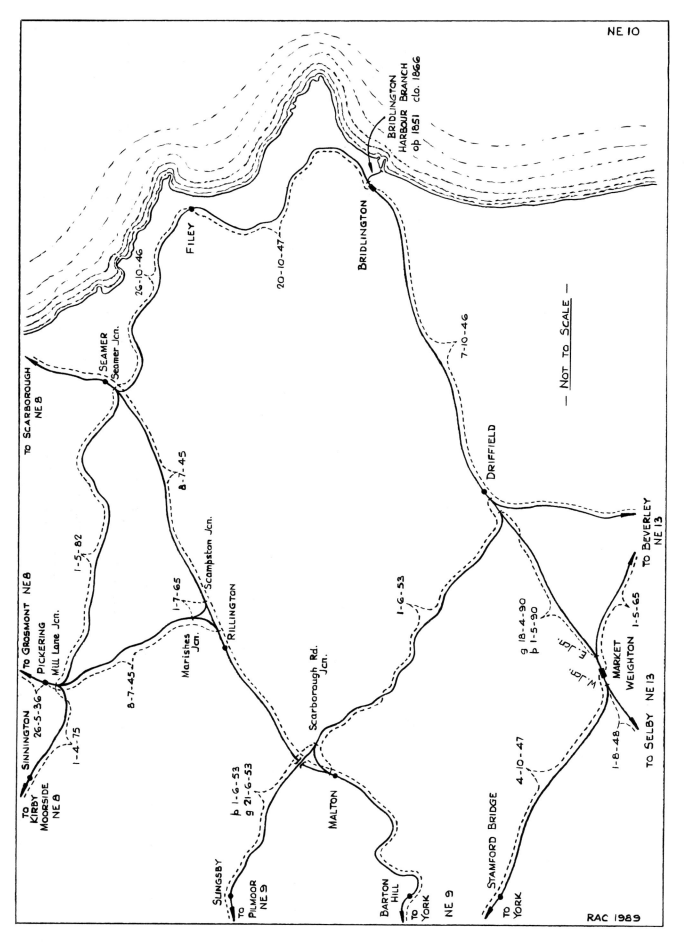

NE 10

BRIDLINGTON HARBOUR BRANCH clo. 1866
op 1851

BRIDLINGTON

FILEY

26-10-46

20-10-47

7-10-46

— NOT TO SCALE —

SEAMER
Seamer Jcn.

TO SCARBOROUGH
NE 8

DRIFFIELD

8-7-45

1-5-82

Scampston Jcn.

1-7-65

RILLINGTON

1-6-53

TO GROSMONT NE 8

PICKERING
Mill Lane Jcn.

Marishes Jcn.

Scarborough Rd. Jcn.

g 18-4-90
p 1-5-90

TO BEVERLEY
NE 13

1-5-65

W. & G.

TO SINNINGTON
26-5-36

8-7-45

MARKET WEIGHTON
NE 13

TO KIRBY
MOORSIDE
NE 8

1-4-75

p 1-6-53
g 21-6-53

MALTON

4-10-47

1-8-48

TO SELBY NE 13

SLINGSBY

TO
PILMOOR
NE 9

BARTON HILL

TO
YORK

NE 9

STAMFORD BRIDGE

TO
YORK

RAC 1989

34

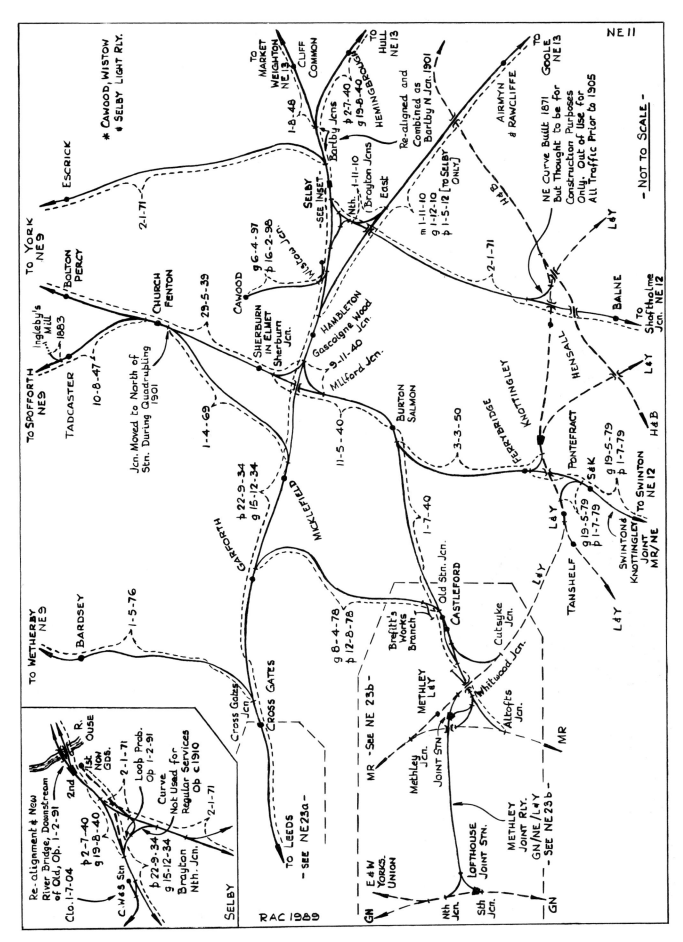

NE 11

- NOT TO SCALE -

RAC 1989

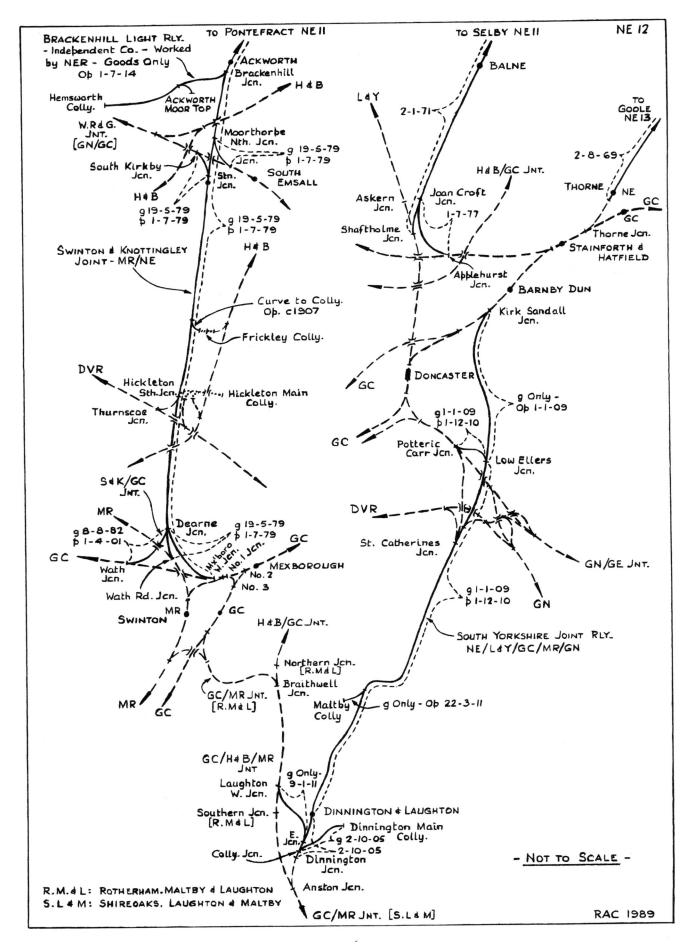

NE 12

BRACKENHILL LIGHT RLY.
- Independent Co. - Worked
by NER - Goods Only
Op 1-7-14

TO PONTEFRACT NE 11

TO SELBY NE 11

ACKWORTH
Brackenhill
Jcn.

Hemsworth
Colly.

ACKWORTH
MOOR TOP

H & B

W.R & G.
JNT.
[GN/GC]

Moorthorpe
Nth. Jcn.

g 19-5-79
p 1-7-79

South Kirkby
Jcn.

Stn.
Jcn.

SOUTH
EMSALL

H & B

g 19-5-79
p 1-7-79

g 19-5-79
p 1-7-79

H & B

SWINTON & KNOTTINGLEY
JOINT - MR/NE

Curve to Colly.
Op c1907

Frickley Colly.

DVR

Hickleton
Sth. Jcn.

Hickleton Main
Colly.

Thurnscoe
Jcn.

S & K/GC
JNT.

MR

g 8-8-82
p 1-4-01

GC

Dearne
Jcn.

g 19-5-79
p 1-7-79

GC

Mx'boro
W. Jcn.

No.1 Jcn.

MEXBOROUGH

Wath
Jcn.

No. 2

No. 3

Wath Rd. Jcn.

SWINTON

MR

GC

H & B/GC JNT.

MR

GC

Northern Jcn.
[R.M & L]

Braithwell
Jcn.

GC/MR JNT.
[R.M & L]

Maltby
Colly.

g Only - Op 22-3-11

GC/H & B/MR
JNT

Laughton
W. Jcn.

g Only -
9-1-11

Southern Jcn.
[R.M & L]

DINNINGTON & LAUGHTON

Dinnington Main
Colly.

g 2-10-05

E.
Jcn.

2-10-05

Colly. Jcn.

Dinnington
Jcn.

Anston Jcn.

GC/MR JNT. [S.L & M]

L & Y

2-1-71

Askern
Jcn.

Shaftholme
Jcn.

Joan Croft
Jcn.

1-7-77

H & B/GC JNT.

Applehurst
Jcn.

BALNE

TO
GOOLE
NE 13

2-8-69

THORNE

NE

GC

GC

Thorne Jcn.

STAINFORTH &
HATFIELD

BARNBY DUN

Kirk Sandall
Jcn.

GC

DONCASTER

g Only -
Op 1-1-09

GC

g 1-1-09
p 1-12-10

Potteric
Carr Jcn.

Low Ellers
Jcn.

DVR

St. Catherines
Jcn.

GN/GE JNT.

g 1-1-09
p 1-12-10

GN

SOUTH YORKSHIRE JOINT RLY.
NE/L & Y/GC/MR/GN

- NOT TO SCALE -

R.M & L: ROTHERHAM, MALTBY & LAUGHTON
S.L & M: SHIREOAKS, LAUGHTON & MALTBY

RAC 1989

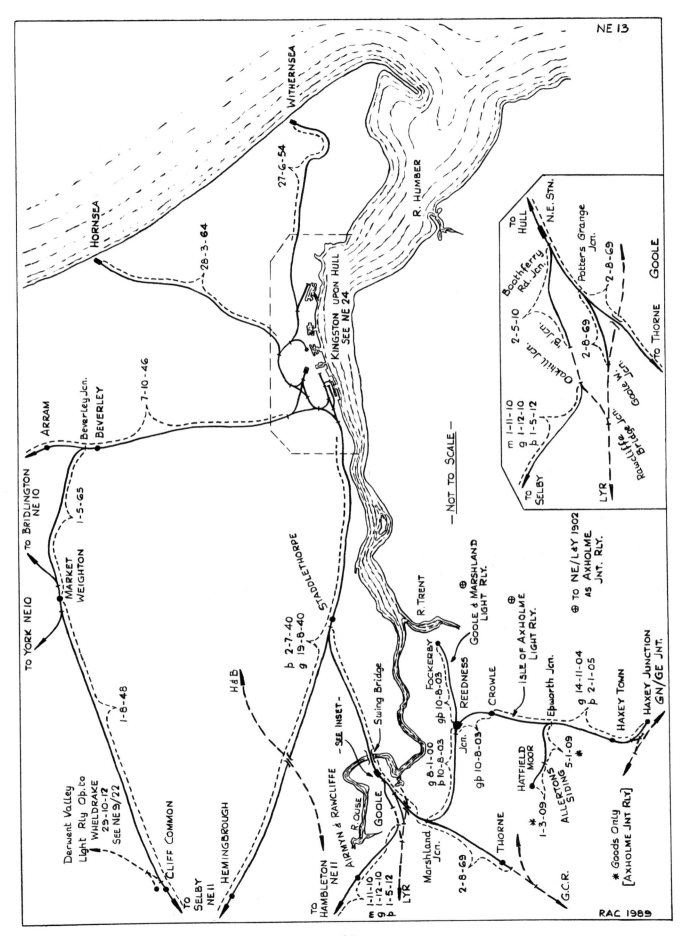

NE 13

R. HUMBER

WITHERNSEA

27-6-54

HORNSEA

28-3-64

ARRAM

Beverley Jcn.
BEVERLEY

7-10-46

TO BRIDLINGTON
NE 11

1-5-65

TO YORK NE 10

MARKET
WEIGHTON

KINGSTON UPON HULL
SEE NE 24

1-8-48

Derwent Valley
Light Rly Op. to
WHELDRAKE
29-10-12
SEE NE 9/22

CLIFF COMMON

To
SELBY
NE 11

HEMINGBROUGH

H & B

STADDLETHORPE

p 2-7-40
g 19-8-40

R. TRENT

R. OUSE
GOOLE

Swing Bridge

SEE INSET

TO
HAMBLETON
NE 11

AIRMYN & RAWCLIFFE

m 1-11-10
g 1-12-10
p 1-5-12
LYR

Marshland
Jcn.

2-8-69

THORNE

g 8-1-00
p 10-8-03

Jcn.

gp 10-8-03

FOCKERBY

gp 10-8-03

REEDNESS

Goole & Marshland
Light Rly.

CROWLE

ISLE OF AXHOLME
LIGHT RLY.

⊕

Epworth Jcn.

HATFIELD
MOOR

* 1-3-09

ALLERTONS
SIDING 5-1-09

g 14-11-04
p 2-1-05

HAXEY TOWN

HAXEY JUNCTION
GN/GE JNT.

⊕ TO NE/L&Y 1902
AS AXHOLME
JNT. RLY.

* Goods Only
[AXHOLME JNT RLY]

G.C.R.

RAC 1989

— NOT TO SCALE —

To
HULL

N.E. STN.

Boothferry
Rd. Jcn.

2-5-10

Oakhill Jcn.

B. Jcn.

m 1-11-10
g 1-12-10
p 1-5-12

To
SELBY

LYR

Potters Grange
Jcn.

2-8-69

2-8-69

Goole Jcn.

Rawcliffe Bridge Jcn.

TO THORNE   GOOLE

37

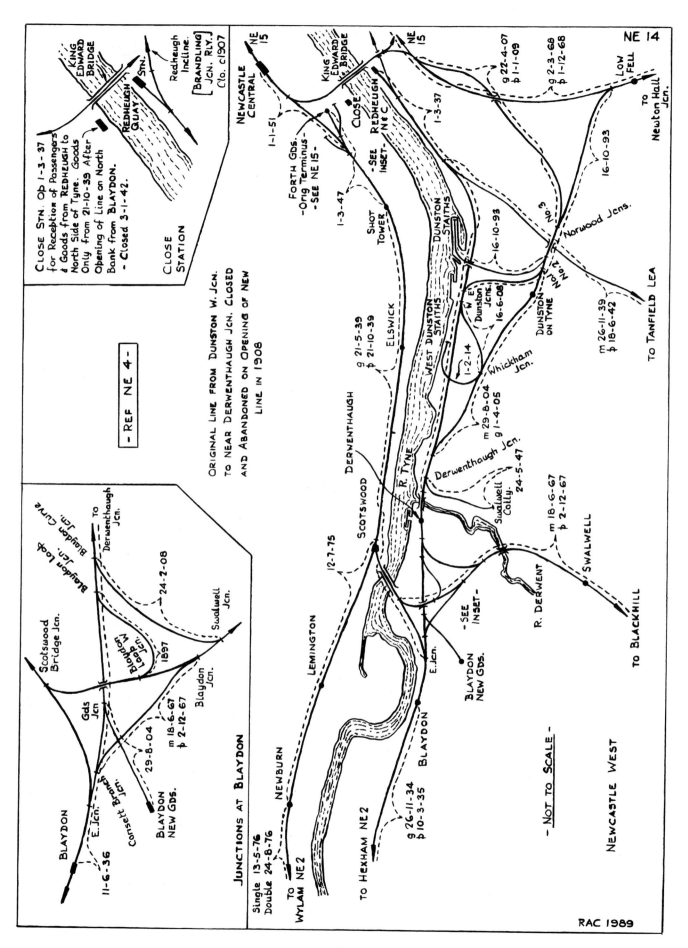

CLOSE STATION

CLOSE STN. OP 1-3-37 for Reception of Passengers & Goods from REDHEUGH to North Side of Tyne. Goods Only from 21-10-39 After Opening of Line on North Bank from BLAYDON. - Closed 3-1-42.

[BRANDLING JCN. RLY.] Clo. c1907

Redheugh Incline.

REDHEUGH QUAY STN.

KING EDWARD BRIDGE

- REF NE 4 -

ORIGINAL LINE FROM DUNSTON W. JCN. TO NEAR DERWENTHAUGH JCN. CLOSED AND ABANDONED ON OPENING OF NEW LINE IN 1908

JUNCTIONS AT BLAYDON

To Derwenthaugh Jcn.

Blaydon Curve

Scotswood Bridge Jcn.

Blaydon Loop Jcn.

24-2-08

1897

Swalwell Jcn.

Gds. Jcn.

29-8-04

m 18-6-67
ϕ 2-12-67

Blaydon Jcn.

BLAYDON

E. Jcn.

Consett Branch Jcn.

11-6-36

BLAYDON NEW GDS.

Single 13-5-76
Double 24-8-76

NEWBURN

TO WYLAM NE 2

LEMINGTON

SCOTSWOOD

DERWENTHAUGH

R. TYNE

12-7-75

g 21-5-39
ϕ 21-10-39

ELSWICK

SHOT TOWER

1-3-47

FORTH GDS. -Orig Terminus- -SEE NE 15-

1-1-51

NEWCASTLE CENTRAL

NE 15

KING EDWARD BRIDGE

NE 15

CLOSE

REDHEUGH N&C - SEE INSET -

1-3-37

16-10-93

WEST DUNSTON STAITHS

DUNSTON STAITHS

1-2-14

W E Dunston Jcn.

16-6-08

Whickham Jcn.

DUNSTON ON TYNE

No. 7

No. 2

No. 3

Norwood Jcns.

16-10-93

g 22-4-07
ϕ 1-1-09

g 2-3-68
ϕ 1-12-68

LOW FELL

TO Newton Hall Jcn.

m 26-11-39
ϕ 18-6-42

TO TANFIELD LEA

m 29-8-04
g 1-4-05

Derwenthaugh Jcn.

Swalwell Colly.

24-5-47

m 18-6-67
ϕ 2-12-67

SWALWELL

R. DERWENT

TO BLACKHILL

- SEE INSET -

BLAYDON NEW GDS.

E. Jcn.

BLAYDON

g 26-11-34
ϕ 10-3-35

TO HEXHAM NE 2

NEWCASTLE WEST

- NOT TO SCALE -

RAC 1989

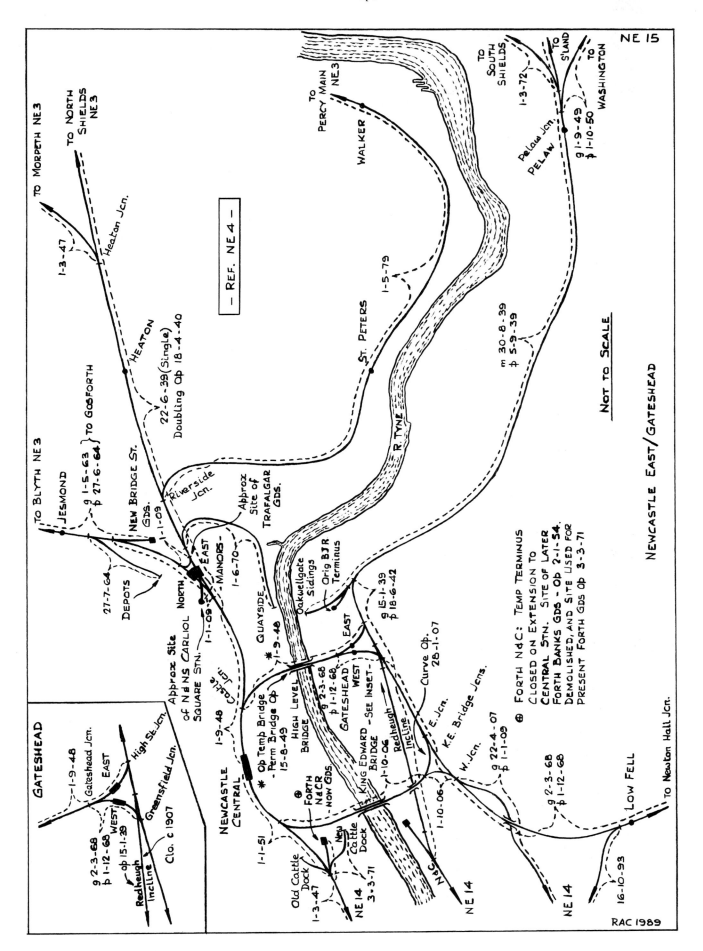

NE 15

- REF. NE 4 -

TO MORPETH NE3

TO NORTH SHIELDS NE3

TO PERCY MAIN NE3

TO SOUTH SHIELDS

TO S'LAND

TO WASHINGTON

WALKER

1-3-72

Pelaw Jcn.

PELAW

o 1-9-49
φ 1-10-50

Heaton Jcn.

1-3-47

HEATON

22-6-39 (Single)
Doubling Op 18-4-40

St. PETERS

1-5-79

R. TYNE

m 30-8-39
φ 5-9-39

TO BLYTH NE3

JESMOND

o 1-5-63
φ 27-6-64 } TO GOSFORTH

NEW BRIDGE St.
GDS. 1-09

Riverside Jcn.

Approx Site of TRAFALGAR GDS.

27-7-64

DEPOTS

EAST
1-1-09

MANORS
1-6-70

Approx Site of N&NS CARLIOL North SQUARE STN.

QUAYSIDE

Oakwellgate Sidings

Orig BJR Terminus

EAST

o 15-1-39
φ 18-6-42

Op Temp Bridge
- Perm Bridge Op
15-8-49

HIGH LEVEL BRIDGE

o 2-3-68
φ 1-12-68

GATESHEAD WEST
- SEE INSET -

Curve Op.
28-1-07

E. Jcn.

K.E. Bridge Jcns.

⊕ FORTH N&C: TEMP TERMINUS
CLOSED ON EXTENSION TO
CENTRAL STN. SITE OF LATER
FORTH BANKS GDS - Op 2-1-54.
DEMOLISHED, AND SITE USED FOR
PRESENT FORTH GDS Op 3-3-71

NEWCASTLE CENTRAL

1-9-48

CASTLE

⊛ 1-9-48

KING EDWARD BRIDGE
1-10-06

Redheugh Incline

W. Jcn.

o 22-4-07
φ 1-1-09

o 2-3-68
φ 1-12-68

1-10-06

LOW FELL

FORTH N&C NOW GDS.

1-1-51

Old Cattle Dock
1-3-47

New Cattle Dock
3-3-71

N&C

NE14

NE14

NE14

16-10-93

TO NEWTON HALL Jcn.

GATESHEAD

1-9-48

Gateshead Jcn.

High St. Jcn.

EAST

o 2-3-68
φ 1-12-68

WEST

op 15-1-39

Greensfield Jcn.

Redheugh Incline

Clo. c 1907

NOT TO SCALE

NEWCASTLE EAST/GATESHEAD

RAC 1989

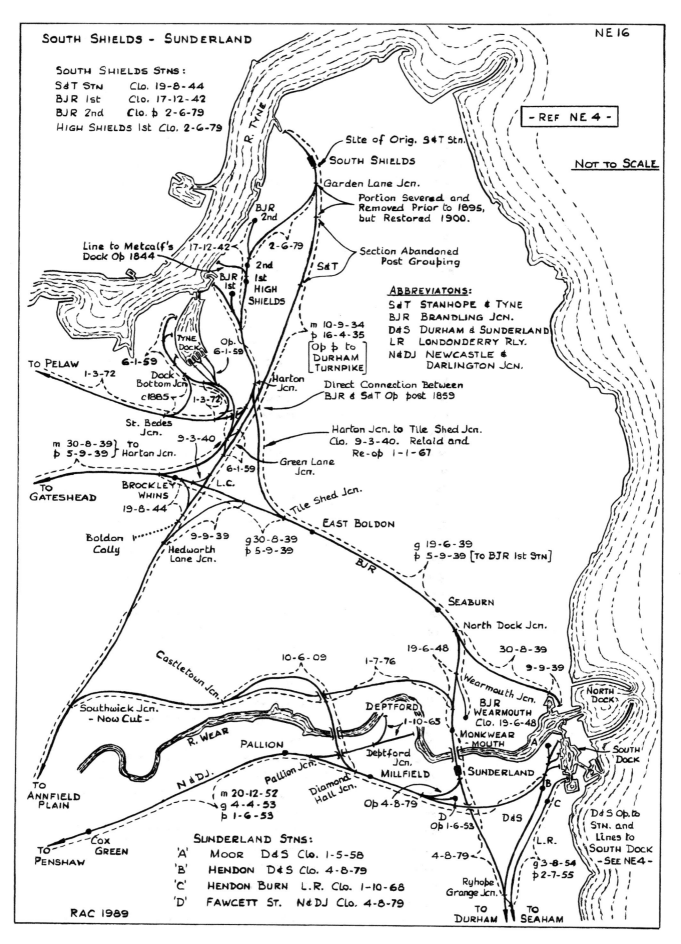

SOUTH SHIELDS - SUNDERLAND

NE 16

SOUTH SHIELDS STNS:
S&T STN   Clo. 19-8-44
BJR 1st   Clo. 17-12-42
BJR 2nd   Clo. þ 2-6-79
HIGH SHIELDS 1st Clo. 2-6-79

- REF NE 4 -

NOT TO SCALE

R. TYNE

Site of Orig. S&T Stn.
SOUTH SHIELDS
Garden Lane Jcn.
Portion Severed and
Removed Prior to 1895,
but Restored 1900.
Section Abandoned
Post Grouping

BJR 2nd

Line to Metcalf's   17-12-42
Dock Op 1844
2nd   2-6-79
1st   S&T
HIGH
BJR 1st   SHIELDS

ABBREVIATONS:
S&T STANHOPE & TYNE
BJR BRANDLING JCN.
D&S DURHAM & SUNDERLAND
LR LONDONDERRY RLY.
N&DJ NEWCASTLE & DARLINGTON JCN.

TYNE DOCK   Op. 6-1-59
TO PELAW   6-1-59
1-3-72
Dock Bottom Jcn.   Harton Jcn.
c1885   1-3-72
St. Bedes Jcn.
9-3-40
m 30-8-39} To
þ 5-9-39 } Harton Jcn.   6-1-59
Green Lane Jcn.
L.C.
TO GATESHEAD
BROCKLEY WHINS
19-8-44

m 10-9-34
þ 16-4-35
Op þ to
DURHAM TURNPIKE

Direct Connection Between
BJR & S&T Op post 1859

Harton Jcn. to Tile Shed Jcn.
Clo. 9-3-40. Relaid and
Re-op 1-1-67

Tile Shed Jcn.
EAST BOLDON

Boldon Colly
9-9-39   g30-8-39
þ 5-9-39
Hedworth Lane Jcn.

g 19-6-39
þ 5-9-39 [TO BJR 1st STN]

BJR

SEABURN
North Dock Jcn.
19-6-48   30-8-39
9-9-39

Castletown Jcn.   10-6-09   1-7-76
Southwick Jcn.
- Now Cut -
R. WEAR   PALLION
Wearmouth Jcn.
NORTH DOCK
BJR WEARMOUTH Clo. 19-6-48
MONKWEAR- MOUTH
A
SOUTH DOCK

DEPTFORD
1-10-65
Deptford Jcn.
MILLFIELD

TO ANNFIELD PLAIN   N&DJ.
Pallion Jcn.
Diamond Hall Jcn.
m 20-12-52
g 4-4-53
þ 1-6-53
Op 4-8-79
D
Op 1-6-53
SUNDERLAND
B
C
D&S
L.R.

D&S Op. to
STN. and
Lines to
SOUTH DOCK
- SEE NE 4 -

Cox GREEN
TO PENSHAW

SUNDERLAND STNS:
'A' MOOR   D&S Clo. 1-5-58
'B' HENDON   D&S Clo. 4-8-79
'C' HENDON BURN L.R. Clo. 1-10-68
'D' FAWCETT ST. N&DJ Clo. 4-8-79

4-8-79
Ryhope Grange Jcn.
TO DURHAM   TO SEAHAM
g 3-8-54
þ 2-7-55

RAC 1989

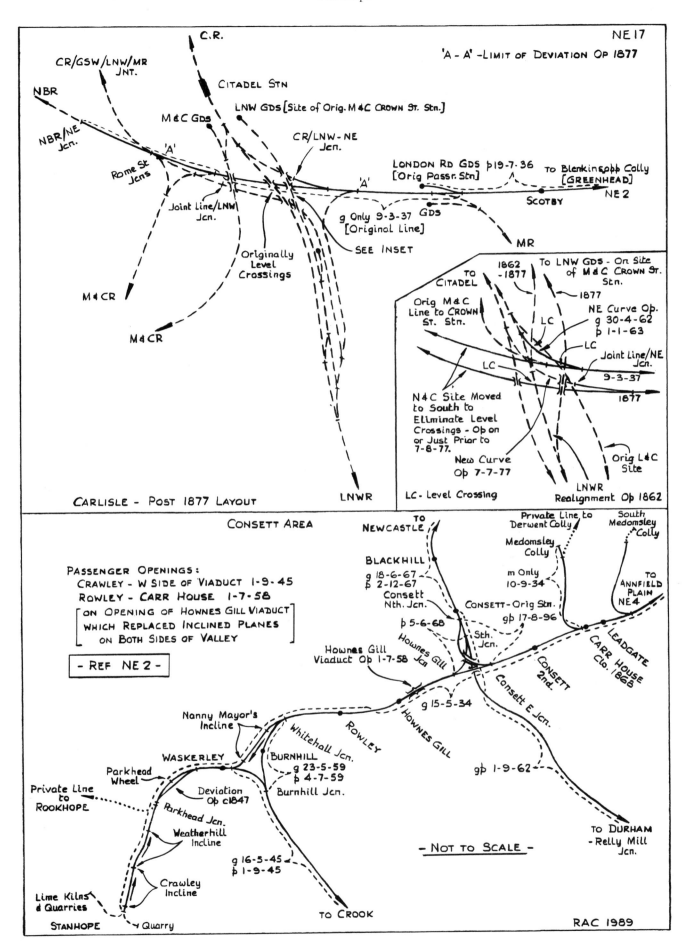

NE 17

'A - A' - LIMIT OF DEVIATION Op 1877

C.R.

CR/GSW/LNW/MR JNT.

CITADEL STN

NBR

LNW GDS [Site of Orig. M&C CROWN ST. STN.]

M&C GDS

NBR/NE Jcn.

CR/LNW-NE Jcn.

'A'

Rome St Jcns

LONDON RD GDS þ19·7·36 [Orig Passr. Stn]

To Blenkinsopp Colly [GREENHEAD]

NE 2

'A'

Joint Line/LNW Jcn.

SCOTBY

Originally Level Crossings

g Only 9-3-37 GDS [Original Line]

MR

M&CR

SEE INSET

M&CR

1862 -1877

To LNW GDS - On Site of M&C CROWN ST. Stn.

TO CITADEL

1877

Orig M&C Line to CROWN ST. Stn.

LC

NE Curve Op. g 30-4-62 þ 1-1-63

LC

Joint Line/NE Jcn.

LC

9-3-37

1877

N&C Site Moved to South to Eliminate Level Crossings - Op on or Just Prior to 7-8-77.

New Curve Op 7-7-77

Orig L&C Site

LNWR

LNWR Realignment Op 1862

CARLISLE - POST 1877 LAYOUT

LC- Level Crossing

CONSETT AREA

TO NEWCASTLE

Private Line to Derwent Colly

South Medomsley Colly

BLACKHILL

Medomsley Colly

PASSENGER OPENINGS:
CRAWLEY - W SIDE OF VIADUCT 1-9-45
ROWLEY - CARR HOUSE 1-7-58

[ON OPENING OF HOWNES GILL VIADUCT
WHICH REPLACED INCLINED PLANES
ON BOTH SIDES OF VALLEY]

g 18-6-67 þ 2-12-67

m Only 10-9-34

TO ANNFIELD PLAIN NE 4

Consett Nth. Jcn.

Consett-Orig Stn.

- REF NE 2 -

þ 5-6-68

gþ 17-8-96

Sth. Jcn.

LEADGATE

CARR HOUSE Clo. 1868

Hownes Gill Viaduct Op 1-7-58

Hownes Gill Jcn.

Consett 2nd.

Consett E Jcn.

g 15-5-34

Nanny Mayor's Incline

Rowley

Hownes Gill

WASKERLEY

Whitehall Jcn.

Parkhead Wheel

BURNHILL g 23-5-59 þ 4-7-59

gþ 1-9-62

Private Line to ROOKHOPE

Deviation Op c1847

Parkhead Jcn.

Burnhill Jcn.

Weatherhill Incline

TO DURHAM - Relly Mill Jcn.

Crawley Incline

g 16-5-45 þ 1-9-45

- NOT TO SCALE -

Lime Kilns & Quarries

STANHOPE

Quarry

TO CROOK

RAC 1989

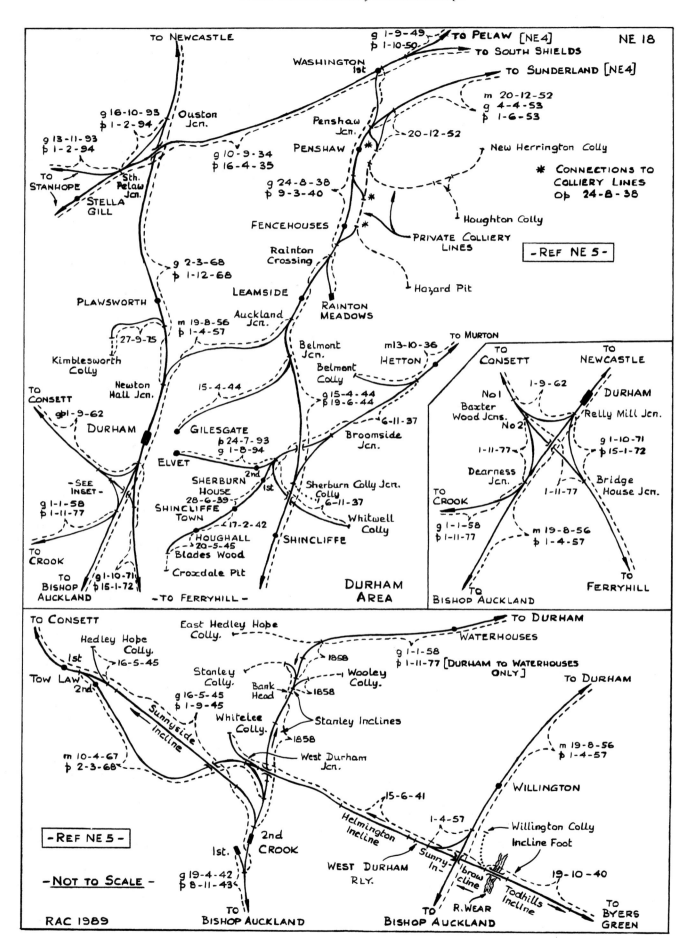

NE 18

TO NEWCASTLE

g 1-9-49 TO PELAW [NE4]
p 1-10-50 TO SOUTH SHIELDS

WASHINGTON 1st

TO SUNDERLAND [NE4]

m 20-12-52
g 4-4-53
p 1-6-53

g 16-10-93 Ouston Jcn.
p 1-2-94

Penshaw Jcn.

20-12-52

g 13-11-93
p 1-2-94

PENSHAW

New Herrington Colly.

TO STANHOPE

Sth. Pelaw Jcn.

STELLA GILL

g 10-9-34
p 16-4-35

g 24-8-38
p 9-3-40

✱ CONNECTIONS TO COLLIERY LINES op 24-8-38

Houghton Colly.

FENCEHOUSES

PRIVATE COLLIERY LINES

-REF NE 5-

Rainton Crossing

g 2-3-68
p 1-12-68

Hazard Pit

LEAMSIDE

PLAWSWORTH

Auckland Jcn.

RAINTON MEADOWS

m 19-8-56
p 1-4-57

TO MURTON

Belmont Jcn.

m 13-10-36

27-9-75

Belmont Colly.

HETTON

Kimblesworth Colly.

Newton Hall Jcn.

15-4-44

g 15-4-44
p 19-6-44

TO CONSETT

TO NEWCASTLE

No1 Baxter Wood Jcns.

1-9-62

DURHAM

Relly Mill Jcn.

TO CONSETT

6-11-37

No 2.

g 1-9-62

DURHAM

GILESGATE

Broomside Jcn.

g 1-10-71
p 15-1-72

p 24-7-93
g 1-8-94

1-11-77

Dearness Jcn.

Bridge House Jcn.

ELVET

2nd

-SEE INSET-

SHERBURN HOUSE

1st

Sherburn Colly Jcn.

Colly

g 1-1-58
p 1-11-77

28-6-39

6-11-37

1-11-77

SHINCLIFFE TOWN

17-2-42

Whitwell Colly

g 1-1-58
p 1-11-77

TO CROOK

HOUGHALL

SHINCLIFFE

20-5-45

Blades Wood

m 19-8-56
p 1-4-57

TO BISHOP AUCKLAND

g 1-10-71
p 15-1-72

Croxdale Pit

DURHAM AREA

TO FERRYHILL

TO BISHOP AUCKLAND

TO FERRYHILL

-TO FERRYHILL-

TO CONSETT

East Hedley Hope Colly.

TO DURHAM

WATERHOUSES

Hedley Hope Colly.

16-5-45

1858

g 1-1-58
p 1-11-77 [DURHAM TO WATERHOUSES ONLY]

TOW LAW

1st

Stanley Colly.

Wooley Colly.

2nd

Bank Head

1858

Sunnyside Incline

g 16-5-45
p 1-9-45

TO DURHAM

Stanley Inclines

Whitelee Colly.

m 10-4-67
p 2-3-68

1858

West Durham Jcn.

m 19-8-56
p 1-4-57

15-6-41

WILLINGTON

Helmington Incline

1-4-57

Willington Colly. Incline Foot

-REF NE 5-

2nd CROOK

WEST DURHAM RLY.

Sunny-In-

brow Icline

19-10-40

-NOT TO SCALE-

1st.

Todhills Incline

g 19-4-42
p 8-11-43

TO BISHOP AUCKLAND

R. WEAR

TO BISHOP AUCKLAND

TO BYERS GREEN

RAC 1989

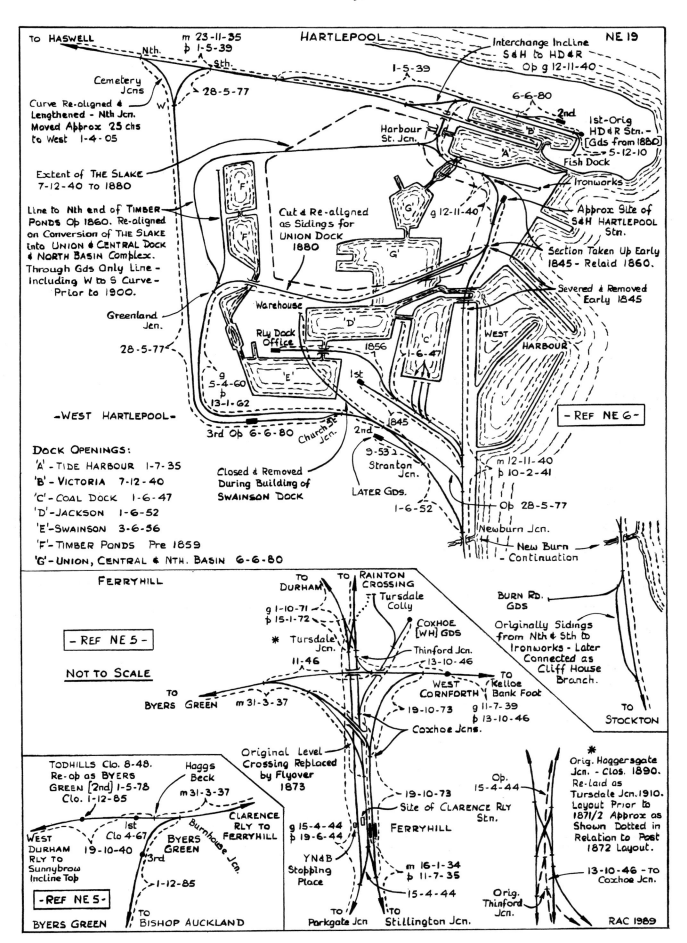

NE 19

TO HASWELL

m 23-11-35
þ 1-5-39

HARTLEPOOL

Interchange Incline
S&H to HD&R
Op g 12-11-40

Nth.

1st-Orig
HD&R Stn. -
[Gds from 1880]
5-12-10

1-5-39

Sth.

6-6-80

2nd

Cemetery Jcns

28-5-77

Fish Dock

Curve Re-aligned &
Lengthened - Nth Jcn.
Moved Approx 25 chs
to West 1-4-05

W

Harbour
St. Jcn.

Ironworks

A

B

G

Approx Site of
S&H HARTLEPOOL
Stn.

Extent of THE SLAKE
7-12-40 to 1880

F

Cut & Re-aligned
as Sidings for
UNION DOCK
1880

g 12-11-40

G

Section Taken Up Early
1845 - Relaid 1860.

Line to Nth end of TIMBER
PONDS Op 1860. Re-aligned
on Conversion of THE SLAKE
into UNION & CENTRAL DOCK
& NORTH BASIN Complex.
Through Gds Only Line -
Including W to S Curve -
Prior to 1900.

F

G

Severed & Removed
Early 1845

Greenland
Jcn.

Warehouse

D

WEST
HARBOUR

28-5-77

Rly Dock
Office

1856

C

E

1st

1-6-47

-WEST HARTLEPOOL-

g
5-4-60
þ
13-1-62

Y
1845

- REF NE 6 -

DOCK OPENINGS:

'A' - TIDE HARBOUR 1-7-35

'B' - VICTORIA 7-12-40

'C' - COAL DOCK 1-6-47

'D' - JACKSON 1-6-52

'E' - SWAINSON 3-6-56

'F' - TIMBER PONDS Pre 1859

'G' - UNION, CENTRAL & NTH. BASIN 6-6-80

3rd Op 6-6-80

Church St. Jcn.

2nd

9-53

Stranton
Jcn.

LATER GDS.

1-6-52

Closed & Removed
During Building of
SWAINSON DOCK

m 12-11-40
þ 10-2-41

Op 28-5-77

Newburn Jcn.

New Burn
- Continuation

BURN RD.
GDS

Originally Sidings
from Nth & Sth to
Ironworks - Later
Connected as
Cliff House
Branch.

FERRYHILL

TO
DURHAM

TO RAINTON
CROSSING

Tursdale
Colly

g 1-10-71
þ 15-1-72

COXHOE
[WH] GDS

- REF NE 5 -

* Tursdale
Jcn.

Thinford Jcn.
13-10-46

NOT TO SCALE

11-46

WEST
CORNFORTH

TO
Kelloe
Bank Foot

TO
BYERS GREEN

m 31-3-37

19-10-73

g 11-7-39
þ 13-10-46

TO
STOCKTON

Coxhoe Jcns.

Original Level
Crossing Replaced
by Flyover
1873

19-10-73

Op.
15-4-44

* Orig. Haggersgate
Jcn. - Clos. 1890.
Re-laid as
Tursdale Jcn.1910.
Layout Prior to
1871/2 Approx as
Shown Dotted in
Relation to Post
1872 Layout.

TODHILLS Clo. 8-48.
Re-op as BYERS
GREEN [2nd] 1-5-78
Clo. 1-12-85

HAGGS
BECK
m 31-3-37

CLARENCE
RLY TO
FERRYHILL

Site of CLARENCE RLY
Stn.

g 15-4-44
þ 19-6-44

FERRYHILL

WEST
DURHAM
RLY TO
Sunnybrow
Incline Top

1st
Clo 4-67

19-10-40

Burnhouse Jcn.

BYERS
GREEN

3rd

YN&B
Stopping
Place

m 16-1-34
þ 11-7-35

13-10-46 - TO
Coxhoe Jcn.

Orig.
Thinford
Jcn.

1-12-85

- REF NE 5 -

BYERS GREEN

TO
BISHOP AUCKLAND

15-4-44

TO
Parkgate Jcn.

TO
Stillington Jcn.

RAC 1989

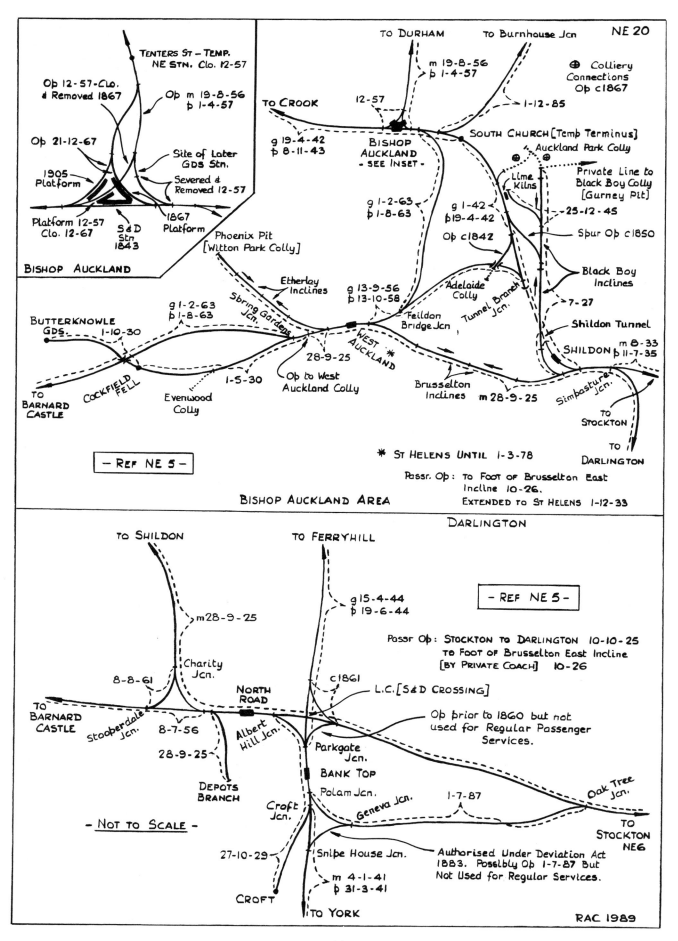

NE 20

BISHOP AUCKLAND (inset)

TENTERS ST — TEMP.
NE STN. CLO. 12-57

Op 12-57-Clo.
d Removed 1867

Op m 19-8-56
þ 1-4-57

Op 21-12-67

Site of Later
GDS Stn.

1905 Platform

Platform 12-57
Clo. 12-67

1867 Platform

S&D Stn 1843

Severed &
Removed 12-57

— REF NE 5 —

TO DURHAM

TO Burnhouse Jcn

m 19-8-56
þ 1-4-57

TO CROOK

12-57

1-12-85

⊕ Colliery Connections
Op c1867

g 19-4-42
þ 8-11-43

BISHOP AUCKLAND - SEE INSET -

SOUTH CHURCH [Temp Terminus]
Auckland Park Colly

Lime Kilns

Private Line to Black Boy Colly [Gurney Pit]

g 1-2-63
þ 1-8-63

g 1-42
þ19-4-42
Op c1842

-25-12-45

Spur Op c1850

Black Boy Inclines

Phoenix Pit [Witton Park Colly]

Etherley Inclines

Spring Gardens Jcn.

g 13-9-56
þ 13-10-58

Adelaide Colly

Tunnel Branch Jcn.

-7-27

Shildon Tunnel

BUTTERKNOWLE GDS.   1-10-30

g 1-2-63
þ 1-8-63

Feildon Bridge Jcn.

WEST AUCKLAND ✱

SHILDON   m 8-33
þ 11-7-35

28-9-25

TO BARNARD CASTLE

COCKFIELD FELL

1-5-30

Op to West Auckland Colly

Evenwood Colly

Brusselton Inclines   m 28-9-25

Simpasture Jcn.

TO STOCKTON

TO DARLINGTON

✱ ST HELENS UNTIL 1-3-78

Passr. Op: To Foot of Brusselton East
Incline 10-26.
Extended to St Helens 1-12-33

BISHOP AUCKLAND AREA

DARLINGTON

TO SHILDON

TO FERRYHILL

— REF NE 5 —

g 15-4-44
þ 19-6-44

Passr Op: Stockton to Darlington 10-10-25
to Foot of Brusselton East Incline
[by Private Coach] 10-26

m 28-9-25

Charity Jcn.

8-8-61

c1861

NORTH ROAD

L.C. [S&D Crossing]

Op prior to 1860 but not
used for Regular Passenger
Services.

TO BARNARD CASTLE

Stooperdale Jcn.

8-7-56

28-9-25

Albert Hill Jcn.

Parkgate Jcn.

BANK TOP

Polam Jcn.

Croft Jcn.

Geneva Jcn.

1-7-87

Oak Tree Jcn.

DEPOTS BRANCH

— NOT TO SCALE —

27-10-29

Snipe House Jcn.

Authorised Under Deviation Act
1883. Possibly Op 1-7-87 But
Not Used for Regular Services.

TO STOCKTON NE6

CROFT

m 4-1-41
þ 31-3-41

TO YORK

RAC 1989

44

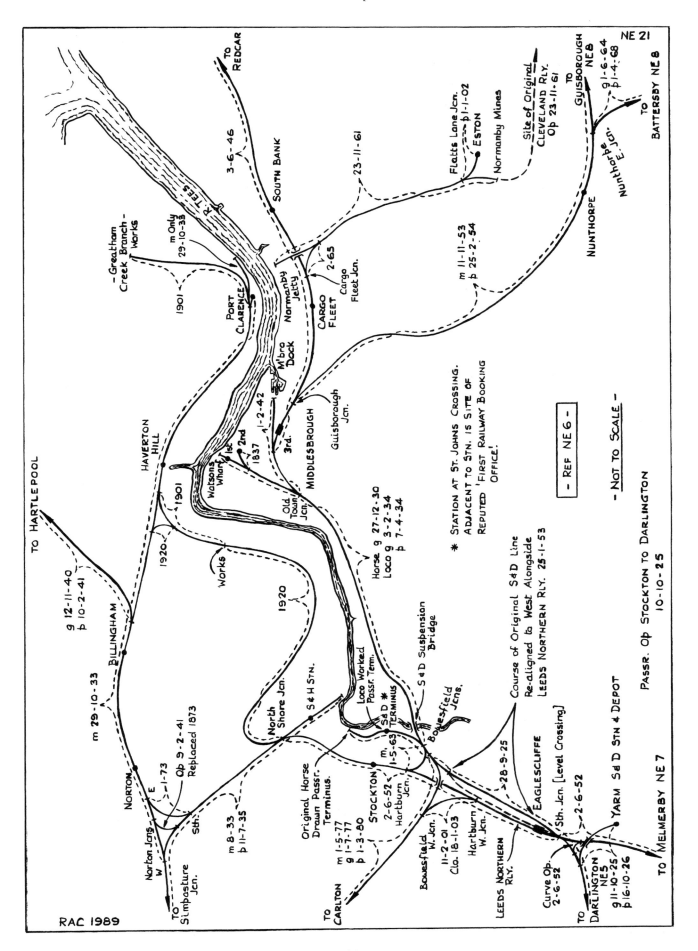

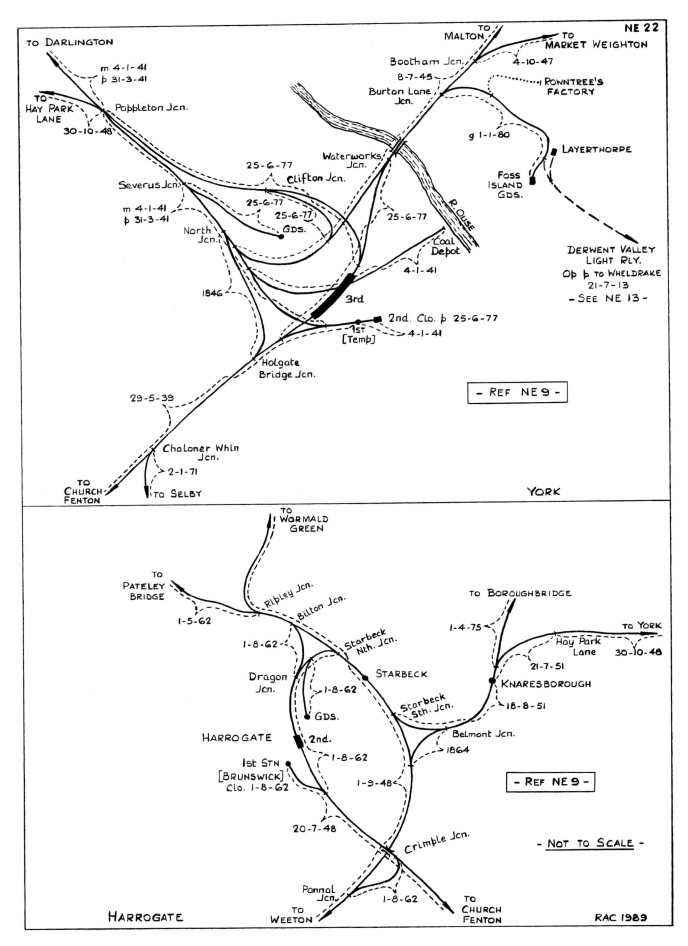

NE 22

TO DARLINGTON

TO MALTON

TO MARKET WEIGHTON
4-10-47

Bootham Jcn.
8-7-45

m 4-1-41
þ 31-3-41

Burton Lane Jcn.

ROWNTREE'S FACTORY

TO HAY PARK LANE

Poppleton Jcn.

30-10-48

Waterworks Jcn.

g 1-1-80

LAYERTHORPE

25-6-77

Clifton Jcn.

Severus Jcn.

25-6-77

GDS.

25-6-77

R. OUSE

FOSS ISLAND GDS.

m 4-1-41
þ 31-3-41

North Jcn.

25-6-77

Coal Depot

DERWENT VALLEY LIGHT RLY.
Op þ to WHELDRAKE
21-7-13
- SEE NE 13 -

1846

4-1-41

3rd

2nd. Clo. þ 25-6-77

1st [Temp]

4-1-41

Holgate Bridge Jcn.

- REF NE 9 -

29-5-39

Chaloner Whin Jcn.

2-1-71

TO CHURCH FENTON

TO SELBY

YORK

TO WORMALD GREEN

TO PATELEY BRIDGE

Ripley Jcn.

Bilton Jcn.

TO BOROUGHBRIDGE

1-5-62

Starbeck Nth. Jcn.

1-4-75

TO YORK

Hay Park Lane

30-10-48

1-8-62

STARBECK

Dragon Jcn.

1-8-62

21-7-51

HARROGATE

GDS.

Starbeck Sth. Jcn.

KNARESBOROUGH

18-8-51

2nd.

Belmont Jcn.

1-8-62

1864

1st STN [BRUNSWICK] Clo. 1-8-62

- REF NE 9 -

1-9-48

20-7-48

Crimble Jcn.

- NOT TO SCALE -

Pannal Jcn.

1-8-62

TO CHURCH FENTON

HARROGATE

TO WEETON

RAC 1989

46

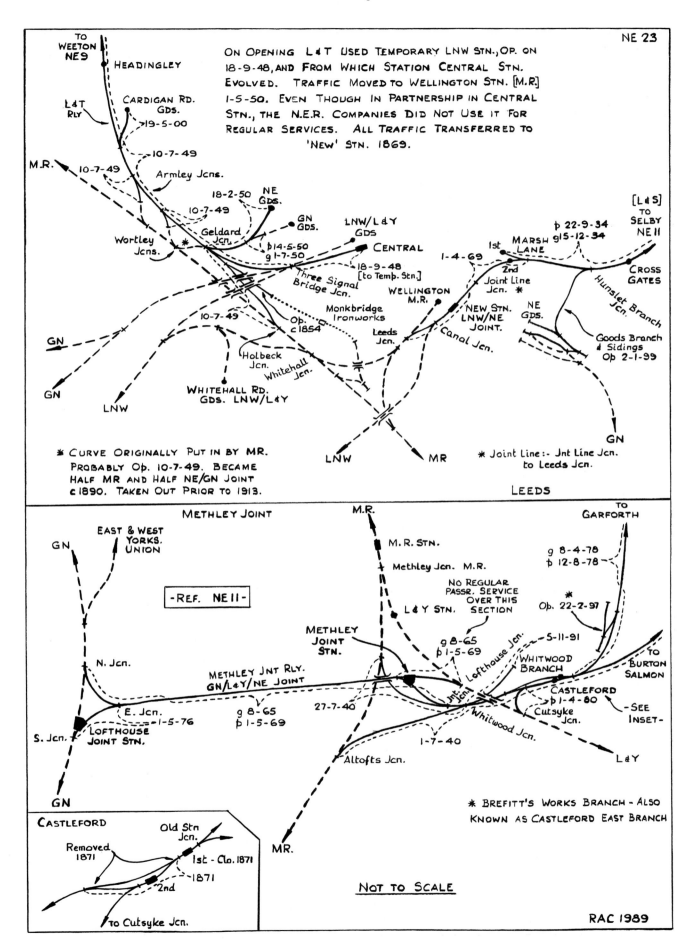

ON OPENING L&T USED TEMPORARY LNW STN., OP. ON 18-9-48, AND FROM WHICH STATION CENTRAL STN. EVOLVED. TRAFFIC MOVED TO WELLINGTON STN. [M.R.] 1-5-50. EVEN THOUGH IN PARTNERSHIP IN CENTRAL STN., THE N.E.R. COMPANIES DID NOT USE IT FOR REGULAR SERVICES. ALL TRAFFIC TRANSFERRED TO 'NEW' STN. 1869.

TO WEETON NE 9

HEADINGLEY

CARDIGAN RD. GDS. 19-5-00

L&T RLY

M.R. 10-7-49

10-7-49

Armley Jcns.

18-2-50

NE GDS.

10-7-49

GN GDS.

LNW/L&Y GDS.

Wortley Jcns.

Geldard Jcn.

14-5-50
1-7-50

CENTRAL

[L&S] TO SELBY NE 11

1st

22-9-34
15-12-34

MARSH LANE

1-4-69

2nd Joint Line Jcn.

CROSS GATES

18-9-48 [to Temp. Stn.]

Three Signal Bridge Jcn.

WELLINGTON M.R.

NEW STN. LNW/NE JOINT.

NE GDS.

Hunslet Branch Jcn.

GN

10-7-49

Monkbridge Ironworks

Op. c1854

Leeds Jcn.

Canal Jcn.

Goods Branch & Sidings Op 2-1-99

GN

Holbeck Jcn.

Whitehall Jcn.

GN

LNW

WHITEHALL RD. GDS. LNW/L&Y

LNW

MR

GN

* CURVE ORIGINALLY PUT IN BY MR. PROBABLY OP. 10-7-49. BECAME HALF MR AND HALF NE/GN JOINT c1890. TAKEN OUT PRIOR TO 1913.

* Joint Line :- Jnt Line Jcn. to Leeds Jcn.

LEEDS

METHLEY JOINT

M.R.

TO GARFORTH

GN

EAST & WEST YORKS. UNION

M.R. STN.

Methley Jcn. M.R.

g 8-4-78
12-8-78

-REF. NE 11-

L&Y STN.

NO REGULAR PASSR. SERVICE OVER THIS SECTION

Op. 22-2-97

N. Jcn.

METHLEY JOINT STN.

METHLEY JNT RLY. GN/L&Y/NE JOINT

g 8-65
1-5-69

Jnt Lofthouse Jcn.

5-11-91

WHITWOOD BRANCH

TO BURTON SALMON

E. Jcn.

1-5-76

g 8-65
1-5-69

27-7-40

Jnt Jcn.

Whitwood Jcn.

CASTLEFORD
1-4-80

Cutsyke Jcn.

-SEE INSET-

S. Jcn.

LOFTHOUSE JOINT STN.

Altofts Jcn.

1-7-40

L&Y

GN

* BREFITT'S WORKS BRANCH - ALSO KNOWN AS CASTLEFORD EAST BRANCH

CASTLEFORD

Old Stn Jcn.

Removed 1871

1st - Clo. 1871

1871

2nd

MR.

NOT TO SCALE

To Cutsyke Jcn.

RAC 1989

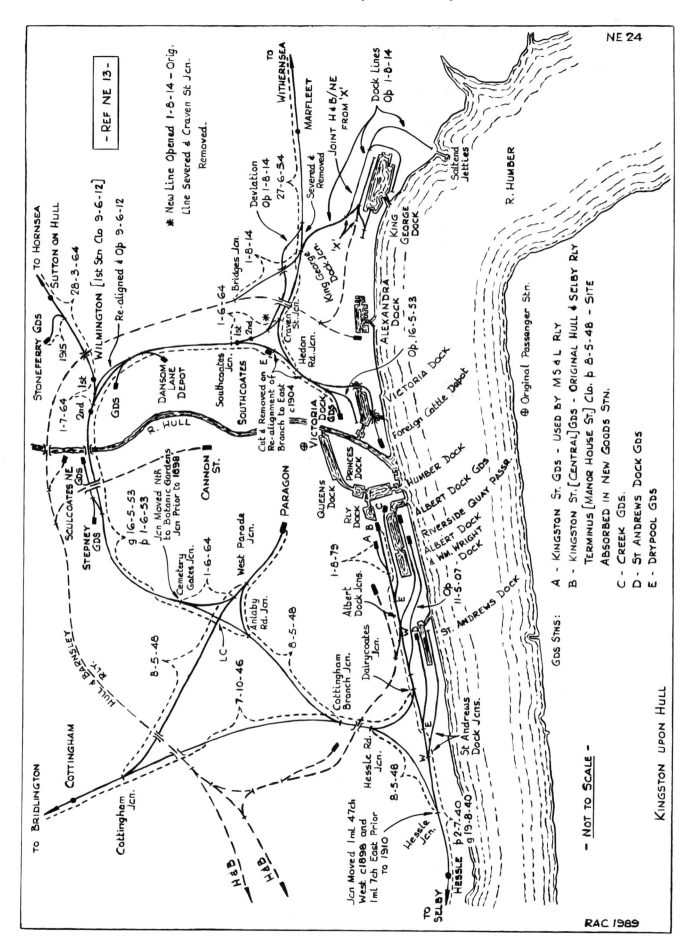

NE 24

- REF NE 13 -

* New Line Opened 1-8-14 - Orig. Line Severed & Craven St Jcn. Removed.

TO HORNSEA
TO WITHERNSEA
MARFLEET
SUTTON ON HULL
28-3-64
STONEFERRY GDS
WILMINGTON [1st Stn Clo 9-6-12]
Re-aligned & Op 9-6-12

Joint H & B/NE FROM 'X'
Dock Lines Op 1-8-14
Severed & Removed
Deviation Op 1-8-14 27-6-54

Bridges Jcn.
1-8-14
King George Dock Jcn. 'X'
KING GEORGE DOCK

1915
1-7-64
2nd 1st

SCULCOATES NE GDS
STEPNEY GDS
R. HULL

DANSOM LANE DEPOT
GDS

Southcoates Jcn.
SOUTHCOATES
1st 2nd
Craven St. Jcn.
Hedon Rd. Jcn.
1-6-64
ALEXANDRA DOCK

Cut & Removed on E Re-alignment of Branch to East c1904
VICTORIA DOCK
Foreign Cattle Depot
Op 16-5-53

g 16-5-53 p 1-6-53
CANNON ST.
Jcn Moved Nth to Botanic Gardens Jcn Prior to 1898

Cemetery Gates Jcn.
1-6-64
West Parade Jcn.
PARAGON
QUEENS DOCK
RLY DOCK
PRINCES DOCK
VICTORIA DOCK GDS
⊕ Original Passenger Stn.

HUMBER DOCK

8-5-48
Anlaby Rd. Jcn.
LC
A B C
ALBERT DOCK GDS
RIVERSIDE QUAY PASSR.
ALBERT DOCK & WM. WRIGHT DOCK

TO COTTINGHAM
TO BRIDLINGTON
Cottingham Jcn.

Cottingham Branch Jcn.
Dairycoates Jcn.
Albert Dock Jcns.
1-8-79
Op 11-5-07
E
ST. ANDREWS DOCK
ST. ANDREWS DOCK

7-10-46

8-5-48
Hessle Rd. Jcn.
St Andrews Dock Jcns.
W E

HULL & BARNSLEY RLY
H & B
H & B

8-5-48
Jcn Moved 1ml 47ch West c1898 and 1ml 7ch East Prior to 1910

HESSLE p 2-7-40 g 19-8-40
Hessle Jcn.

TO SELBY

R. HUMBER
Saltend Jetties

KINGSTON UPON HULL

- NOT TO SCALE -

GDS STNS:
A - KINGSTON ST. GDS - USED BY MS & L RLY
B - KINGSTON ST. [CENTRAL] GDS - ORIGINAL HULL & SELBY RLY TERMINUS [MANOR HOUSE ST.] Clo. p 8-5-48 - SITE ABSORBED IN NEW GOODS STN.
C - CREEK GDS.
D - ST ANDREWS DOCK GDS
E - DRYPOOL GDS

RAC 1989